Literary Creations on the Road

Women's Travel Diaries in Early Modern Japan

Shiba Keiko

Translated with Notes by
Motoko Ezaki

UNIVERSITY PRESS OF AMERICA,® INC.

Lanham • Boulder • New York • Toronto • Plymouth, UK

Contents

Translator's Introduction

Motoko Ezaki

"This is not a thesis, nor did I attempt a new theory or anything so ambitious as to make contributions to academia with this book," states the author Shiba Keiko in her afterword. For years she has searched for materials written by the women of early modern Japan, her quest being to "simply read what they actually wrote" and possibly "learn something universal from them." In spite of her humble statement, this book is an invaluable source of information otherwise unavailable; it offers us a rare window into an unexpected abundance of documentation on travel and writing as undertaken by women in the 17th through mid-19th centuries, when the country was under the rule of the Tokugawa shogunate (also known as the Tokugawa *bakufu*), its political and social systems founded on Neo-Confucianism.

While the officially-sanctioned hierarchical social order of "samurai-peasant-artisan-merchant" was generally observed during the Tokugawa period, the lines of demarcation between the classes were becoming more fluid as time went by.[1] The monetary economy was developing rapidly in the cities, giving rise to the economic power of the merchant class, and the publishing business was flourishing, too. Still, it was predominantly a "man's world" when it came to the authorship of widely distributed popular literature; writings by women of those times have been largely unknown to the general public of the modern era, and are conspicuously absent from many of the standard texts on Japanese literary history. This is in stark contrast to the many works by Heian court ladies of several centuries prior, such as *The Tale of Genji* and *The Pillow Book*, which have enjoyed fame as classic masterpieces with a large corpus of translations and scholarly works dedicated to their study over the centuries. It was often believed that, in the male-dominated society of the Tokugawa period, women did not enjoy the privilege of engaging in the creation of works of literature.

Fortunately, recent scholarship has brought to light a considerable number of works authored by women, thanks to researchers and their untiring efforts.[2] Among these, Shiba's achievement in the current book stands unique by virtue of the sheer number of authors and their journeys that it introduces; her collection of travel diaries had reached nearly two hundred when the book was written, and is a manifestation of her efforts to describe as many works as possible while minimizing her own analytical comments on each text. In her narration she retraces the experiences of each woman, faithfully following the accounts recorded in the travel diaries, and intermittently quotes selections of poetry and prose from the original text, in particular those that capture the traveler's inner processes. After each quotation Shiba briefly paraphrases its content into modern Japanese for the general reader who may have difficulty with the style and diction of the traditional language. With these features the book functions as an excellent guide for the reader who wishes to gain an overview of women and their literary activities of the time, but who, unlike a handful of scholars and trained researchers, rarely has the means to obtain access to those manuscripts, most of which are handwritten and have typically been preserved—in those cases where they were not lost altogether—by the families of these authors' descendants, by local universities, or libraries. For scholars, too, this work can provide a source of inspiration for further research into such little-known authors of Tokugawa Japan. The Japanese original that was first published in 1997 by Yoshikawa Kōbunkan, a well-established Tokyo publisher specializing in academic histories, was reprinted in 2004, indicating the book's appeal to a wide readership.

The main text is divided into four chapters. In the first chapter, which is the longest and comprises half the volume, Shiba categorizes the various women's journeys as being of two types: volitional and compulsory; she then adds a section on the travel of daimyo families. Some women's travels are described in substantial detail while others' are noted quite briefly, depending on the quantity of the source available. In the second chapter, she observes women's travel experiences from three different angles: the difficulties these female travelers faced, the joys of their travel, and what they observed and acquired specifically during their journeys. The third chapter focuses on the cultural and philosophical backgrounds of the traveler/authors, discussing their opportunities for education, the Confucian and National studies that were the two influential learning traditions of the time, and the literary genre *haikai*, which reached the peak of its popularity during the Tokugawa period. The last chapter and the epilogue contemplate how their travel experiences influenced, or possibly changed, the authors' lives after their journeys. Shiba also tells us how those diaries have been handed down for hundreds of years, and ponders the significance of the authors leaving accounts of their travels.

Throughout the chapters, her narration consistently makes reference to relevant parts of the original diaries, with some authors appearing multiple times and others only once or twice.

The women introduced in this book include a certain number of figures whose life and works are well chronicled elsewhere,[3] but the majority are ordinary women from all walks of life, and all social classes. This diversity of women is indeed one important feature of the book, and through it the reader experiences a number of very different women come to life in all their individuality. The same can be said for the men whose trajectories intertwine with those of the female traveler/writers; the reader is likely to have their "old" image of Tokugawa men revised one way or another. This work can thus be appreciated simply as a rich source of information about this historical period in Japan, as has been indicated earlier, while on the other hand it proves to be a clear witness to the unexpectedly high rate of literacy for women and the quality of education during the Tokugawa era, especially its second half, as described as follows: "Noblewomen read and wrote, warrior women read and wrote, commoner women read and wrote, and courtesans . . . read and wrote as well."[4]

Shiba majored in Japan's early modern history at college in the 1960s. While learning, she felt strong doubts about the then-predominant view that the era under the Tokugawa *bakufu* was the darkest time for women, when "the oppression of women marked a nadir in our history."[5] But it was a peaceful time, without wars, that lasted two and a half centuries—thought Shiba; she could not believe that women of the time would acquiesce to such constant subordination for so many years. She began to search for materials written by women themselves, as opposed to the moral texts for women written by men, to gain better knowledge of what they thought and how they actually lived. Her efforts have resulted in a number of publications,[6] as well as forums and lectures that feature the findings of her long-continued research.[7] Still, the popular perception of Tokugawa women, especially outside Japan, may not be very different from that which Shiba encountered during her college days. I hope this English translation of Shiba's book will provide readers with an opportunity to discover a new aspect of women's lives and their place in the literature of early modern Japan.

I would like to express my profound gratitude to Ms. Shiba Keiko for allowing me to translate her work into English. This endeavor has been greatly supported by her enthusiasm and assistance, generously offered no matter how trivial my questions might have been. I would also like to thank a circle of my colleagues at Occidental College, who read excerpts of my translation while still in its early stages, for expressing their genuine interest in its content and warmly encouraging me to continue the project.

I am grateful to my husband Daniel Loeb, for his tireless editing and proof-reading assistance, and my longtime friend Nina Yoshida, a linguist and Japanese studies scholar, for kindly assisting, under tremendous time pressure, my efforts to complete the manuscript, by offering invaluable feedback on both the subject matter and my use of English expressions. Without their support, I could not have finished this work.

NOTES

1. According to Tocco, "the barrier between commoner and samurai was a permeable one—and had been, perhaps, throughout the Tokugawa period." Martha Tocco, "Women's Education in Tokugawa Japan," in *Women and Confucian Cultures in Premodern China, Korea, and Japan*, eds. Dorothy Ko, JaHyun Kim Haboush, and Joan R. Piggott (Berkeley: University of California Press, 2003), p. 210.

2. Among them are Koishi Fusako, *Runin Bōtō-ni* (Sakuhinsha, 2008); Shiba Keiko, *Kinsei no onna tabinikki jiten* (Tokyōdō Shuppan, 2005); Maeda Yoshi, ed., *Kinsei chihō joryū bungei shūi* (Fukuoka: Tsuru Shobō, 2005); Shiba, *Ninomiya Fumi* (Katsura Bunko, 2000); and Kado Reiko, *Edo joryūbungaku no hakken*, (Fujiwara Shoten, 1998), to name a few.

3. In addition to those mentioned in note 2, also note the following: The *kanshi* (Classical Chinese poetry) poet Ema Saikō (1787–1861) had a collection of her poems published posthumously in 1871, entitled *Shōmu ikō*; this collection is fully translated and annotated in Kado's *Ema Saikō shishū "Shōmu ikō"* (Kyūko Shoin,1994). Satō Hiroaki's *Breeze through Bamboo* (New York: Columbia U. Press, 1998) is moreover the English translation of a body of Saikō's works. Patricia Fister's "Female *Bunjin*: The Life of Poet-Painter Ema Saikō," in *Recreating Japanese Women, 1600–1945*, ed. Gail Lee Bernstein (Berkeley: University of California Press, 1991), pp. 108–130, is a critical essay on both her poems and paintings. The life of Matsuo Taseko, the *waka* poet and wife of a village headman, is given a comprehensive biography in Anne Walthall, *The Weak Body of a Useless Woman: Matsuo Taseko and the Meiji Restoration* (Chicago, London: The University of Chicago Press,1998).

4. Tocco, "Women's Education in Tokugawa Japan," p. 197.

5. Takamure Itsue, *Josei no rekishi*, 4 vols. (Kōdansha, 1954–58), page number unknown; quoted in Shiba, *Kinsei onna tabinikki*, (Yoshikawa Kōbunkan, 1997), p.1.

6. In addition to the works published by major publishers, Shiba started a small publishing house, Katsura Bunko, as a venue for introducing written materials of the Tokugawa period that had been discovered and discussed by various people including herself; there, she edited and published a series of journals entitled *Edo-ki onna kō* (Studies on Women of the Tokugawa Period) from 1990 through 2004, whose contributors include scholars from outside Japan as well. Since 1999, Katsura Bunko has been publishing books in a series entitled *Edo-ki hito bunko* (A Library on Tokugawa People).

7. She is portrayed as "a preeminent researcher and editor, who has made invaluable contributions since the 1980s to the study of women's history" by Yabuta Yutaka at the open symposium "Gender and Women's History in the Edo Period," printed in Rikkyo Institute of Japanese Studies Annual Report No. 6, April 2007, p. 20. Not only the depth and breadth of her work but her energetic and holistic approach to life are evident in the recordings of her talks and lectures, including the keynote speech in "*Edo no joseishi fōramu: Osaka*" (The Forum on the History of Tokugawa Women), Kansai University, 2005, pp. 1–12, and a special interview in "*Minshū-shi kenkyūkai kaihō*" (Folk History Conference Newsletter), No. 67, May 2009, pp. 2–8.

Notes on the Translation

All names appearing in the main text of the translation retain the original Japanese order, with the family name given first. Moreover, italics are used to indicate Japanese terms, with the exception of names and those already in common use in English, such as shogun, daimyo, and samurai.

All dates through 1872 are expressed according to the lunar calendar, except the years, for which Shiba provides the conversions to the Gregorian calendar as well; I chose to either spell them out or specify them numerically in the year.month.day format.

The list of references that Shiba cites for her Japanese original are presented separately from the translator's bibliography; the latter documents the references cited by the translator in the Notes section. All notes inserted in the main text have been added by the translator, to provide the reader with supplemental information on the historical context assumed by the Japanese original.

Chapter One

The Reasons Women Traveled

VOLITIONAL TRAVEL

Pilgrimage and Sightseeing

The well over one hundred women's travel diaries from early modern Japan that I have so far collected[1] may be grouped into two broad categories in terms of the purposes and motives for the travel: volitional or compulsory.

Among voluntary journeys, sightseeing trips together with visits to temples and shrines are predominant, accounting for nearly half of all these diaries. The popularity of sightseeing and pilgrimage is apparent from the "Decree of the Keian Era" (*Keian no ofuregaki*) that the Tokugawa government issued in 1649; it dictates in detail daily routines for peasants to observe. Interestingly, the officials felt compelled to add the following provision: "A wife who drinks tea excessively, has a penchant for visiting temples and shrines, and likes to go on outings should be divorced." Nevertheless it did not stop women from taking to the road for excursions and visits to temples and shrines.

Yamanashi Shigako,[2] the housewife and mother of a *sake* brewing family of Iharamura in Suruga province, departed for a pilgrimage to Ise Shrine[3] with her fourth son Tōhei and an attendant in 1792, when she was fifty-five years old. They headed west along the Tōkaidō (a highway),[4] stopped at Mt. Akiha[5] and Hōrai-ji temple,[6] visited both the Inner and Outer Shrines of Ise, and arrived in Kyoto via the Ōmi road. There they watched with amazement the procession of a court aristocrat accompanied by a number of ladies-in-waiting. Passing through Uji, Nara, Yoshino, Mt. Kōya, and Osaka, they viewed the sea of Hyōgo from Mt. Maya. In the Grove of Ikuta, they recalled the historic Genji-Heike battle,[7] then visited the ruins of the Heike clan at Suma and Akashi.

Passing the castle towns of Himeji and Okayama, they reached Marugame in Shikoku[8] by boat. After visiting Konpira Shrine,[9] the party again boarded a boat for Miyajima. During a tour of islands on the Seto Inland Sea,[10] they watched with interest children grazing cows on the grass near the shore of Momoshima. Landing at Hiroshima for the return trip, they visited temples, shrines, and various sights on their way, later resting in Osaka. The party stayed for nearly one month in Kyoto. They apparently saw the famous Kamo Festival and enjoyed other noted events in Kyoto, but their activities are not recorded in her diary, except for the author's simple note that says, "The capital was too splendid for words, and my brush is inadequate for its description." Leaving the city on the thirteenth day of the fifth month, her party passed Fuwa-no-seki and Nagoya, then finally reached Mitsuke (in present-day Shizuoka prefecture) in their home province. From Mitsuke one beheld gorgeous Mt. Fuji (the word *mitsuke* can mean *to view*, hence the town's name). Having thoroughly enjoyed their journey during prime flower season, the second month through the fifth month, Shigako titled her diary "*Haru no michikusa*" (Dawdling along Spring Roads) and concluded it with a *waka*:[11]

> Traveling clothes—
> putting on layers of those for many days
> have I returned home
> and beheld beautiful Fuji,
> What joy, just to hear the name *mitsuke*!

Like Shigako, many women enthusiastically visited famous scenic locations on their way to and from their pilgrimages to Ise Shrine.

Abe Mineko, the matron of the medicine-trading Abe family of Uekimura in Chikuzen province, traveled to Ise Shrine at the age of forty-eight in 1840 and authored a diary entitled "*Ise mōde nikki*" (Diary of a Pilgrimage to Ise). With her friends she left Uekimura on the twenty-third day of the second month and sailed across the Seto Inland Sea to Kyoto. On their way they stopped at Iwakuni, Miyajima, Onomichi, and Okayama to offer prayers at local religious sites. From Marugame they proceeded to visit Konpira Shrine. At Kagaku-ji, a temple remembered for its association with the forty-seven *rōnin* of *Chūshingura* fame,[12] Mineko and her friends were moved to tears by the unveiling of a sacred Buddha. The party then visited Suma-dera temple and the gravesite of Taira no Kiyomori,[13] enjoyed sightseeing in Osaka, and arrived in Kyoto via Uji. They roamed the imperial capital for about ten days and made a tour of the eight famous picturesque spots of Ōmi (known as the *Ōmi hakkei*). At Kusatsu they bought rice cakes called *ubagamochi*, a local specialty of the area, then crossed the mountains of Suzuka heading for Ise Shrine. On their return trip after staying for about three days in Ise, Mineko and her friends crossed the mountains of Iga, toured Nara and Yoshino, then set out to the Seto Inland Sea from Osaka on the second day of the fifth month. They arrived home on the ninth day of the month. It was approximately a forty-day journey.

There were those of strong faith who, often in spite of illness, would embark upon a pilgrimage circuit of holy temples. Iwashita Isoko was the proprietress of a brothel at the Shinagawa post station in Edo. She started her journey to the Chichibu circuit of thirty-three temples accompanied by two attendants in 1860. Isoko, who was of weak constitution, had long been a faithful follower of Kannon Bodhisattva. She departed in a palanquin on the twenty-sixth day of the eighth month and on her way offered prayers at *kishimojin* (the goddess of childbirth and children) in Zōshigaya. In a station at Warabi she saw prostitutes soliciting patrons. The scene must have particularly moved her, being intimately knowledgeable of the lives of such women. Stopping along the way at Ōmiya and Kumagaya, they reached the hot springs of Ikaho.[14] By then, however, Isoko was in poor health, and the party ended up resting there for several days. Afraid of possibly meeting her end in Ikaho, she prayed for the favor of deities and Buddhas. Fortunately she gradually regained her appetite, and they hurried for Chichibu while offering prayers on their way at various temples and shrines. Completing the circuit of Chichibu Kannon temples, the party came home after a seventeen-day journey. The following day Isoko began to write an account of her travel, which was to be completed and entitled "*Chichibu zumrai no ki*" (Pilgrimage to the Chichibu Circuit of Kannon Temples).

Kutsukake Nakako, the mistress of a *sake* brewing house at Sakaki in Shinano province, visited the thirty-four Kannon temples at Chichibu with her third son Engyo[15] and an attendant in 1803, when she was fifty-five years old. They left Sakaki on the fifth day of the third month, taking the reverse route of the circuit, which would normally start from Edo. Stopping at their relatives' homes and family temples on their way, they arrived at the thirty-fourth temple Suisen-ji on the ninth of the month, where they offered prayers to *Senju*-Kannon (Kannon with one-thousand arms). Nakako wrote, "This was the pilgrimage that I had long wished to accomplish, therefore I was determined to go wherever others went and do whatever others could," and indeed she never hesitated to clamber up the hills no matter how steep they were. She obviously embraced the challenges of her life, having shouldered both the family business and the raising of four sons and two daughters after being widowed at the age of forty. Completing her long-cherished pilgrimage, Nakako stopped over at Edo, Enoshima, Kamakura, and Nikkō on her way home. She recorded her accounts of the journey in "*Azumaji no nikki*" (Diary of Traveling East).

Ōkuma Tsugi-jo,[16] the mother of the village headman of Matsudo in Shimōsa province, went on a pilgrimage accompanied by attendants to Chichibu

Kannon and Zenkō-ji[17] at the age of forty-five in 1842, four years after the death of her husband Ihei. Spending seven days (though confined one day in the inn due to snow), they completed the circuit of thirty-four temples, and continued their journey to Zenkō-ji. They rested at the Ikaho hot springs, enjoyed a tour of the lake at Mt. Haruna, and made a circuit of holy temples in Bandō.[18] They extended their journey to Nikkō, Mt. Tsukuba, and Mt. Ashio before returning home to complete their travel after thirty-five days. Her account of the travel "*Chichibu dōchū oboe*" (Notes on a Journey to Chichibu) records not only the temples and shrines they visited and the itinerary of each day but the names of the inns they stayed at as well, some of which are still in business under the same names.

Tsugi-jo traveled again at the age of fifty-one for about twenty days to visit the shrines of Mt. Narita, Katori, and Kashima, as well as some of the thirty-three holy temples in Bandō. Of this travel she left a simple account entitled "*Sansha sankei Chōshi narabini higashi Bandō dōchū-ki*" (Travel to the Three Shrines and the Bandō Circuit).

Presumably Nakako's and Tsugi-jo's pilgrimages were for the repose of their husbands' souls. They were both widowed in their forties, and both retained actual leadership among their respective kin even though they had handed over their family businesses to their sons.

Travel for Learning and Training

Under the Tokugawa *bakuhan* system, where the central Tokugawa government (*bakufu*) and regional domains (*han*) of the daimyo maintained equilibrium in their feudal relationships, there existed strict regulations governing various aspects of life, including the four-tiered samurai-peasant-artisan-merchant class system and the male-dominant nature of society. We may certainly infer that the people enjoyed less freedom and suffered more hardships than we do in our contemporary world. However, the relatively peaceful world that lasted over two hundred years without wars, accelerated by the growth and spread of the monetary economy, diffused culture and education through unprecedentedly vast regions and classes, from well-to-do merchants to ordinary people in the cities, and to wealthy farmers and beyond in the villages. They now had access to education and cultural activities, which had been the province of a handful of privileged people for centuries. People were not only receiving, but actively creating, culture. They often traveled in search of cultural activities instead of waiting for the newest waves to reach them. They traveled not only to the three metropolises, Edo, Kyoto and Osaka, but across the country to socialize with like-minded people of taste. At times they would sojourn for days and weeks for further academic learning or training in the literary arts. Nature was also their teacher, providing the traveler with inspiration for poetry, drawing, and painting. Even during pilgrimage and sightseeing, people engaged in literary creation as they journeyed. Most of the travel diaries I have introduced so far carry a number of *waka* poems interspersed in the text, indicating that composition of poetry was another important purpose of their travel.

It was not only men but women, too, who traveled with their families or by themselves for the purpose of further learning and training.

Pursuit of Literary Art—A Versatile Artist

Being widowed at the age of twenty four, Tagami Kikusha-ni of Chōfu in western Japan returned to her natal family and was reinstated as their daughter. When she was twenty-eight, Kikusha-ni took Buddhist tonsure.[19] At the time, she composed the following *hokku* (a 17-syllable precursor to *haiku*):[20]

> In the autumn winds
> have I shaken the worldly dust
> from my soul and body

The lay nun[21] was refreshed and reinvigorated. She longed for a life devoted to art and poetry, and for escape from the pressures of adhering to the model of feminine virtue that society expected, particularly of young widows and divorcees. In 1780 she left home for poetry training, the first of numerous journeys in search of artistic education she would make throughout her life, accompanied only by a traveling hat and a walking stick. She studied for several months under Chōboen Sankyō,[22] a *haikai*[23] master of the Mino school of Iwatemura in Mino province, and then left for the northern region of Ōshū for further training. In her humble travel sack was her master Sankyō's warm reference letter addressed to his followers across the country. The letter said, "I cordially ask of you to please be kind enough to provide her with one night's accommodation." Still, she could not help but once murmur, "Forlorn and helpless, my solitude extends beyond the horizon."

She traveled along the Hokkoku-kaidō towards Echizen, then in Kaga she visited the cenotaph of the late *haikai* poetess Chiyo-jo. There she paid a courtesy call to Chiyo-jo's adopted son Hakuu to hear his memories of the renowned poetess. Kikusha-ni continued her journey north along the Sea of Japan coast, calling on her *haikai* friends in Kanazawa, Noto, Etchū, and Echigo, and then visited Zenkō-ji to offer prayers. Later she reversed her route towards Oguni in Dewa province in northern Japan, where she received lessons in calligraphy from an expert named Goshō. After that her journey partly followed the route of the revered Bashō's steps,[24] passing through Matsushima, Miyagino, and Nikkō, and finally brought her to Edo at the end of the year. During her two-year stay in this great city, Kikusha-ni participated in poetry meetings and tea ceremonies under the guidance of Sankyō's leading disciple Hakujubō. By then she had made her name as a *haikai* poetess, often invited into the company of high society, including daimyo and court nobles.

"My days are filled with the pleasure of art and poetry, constantly invited by my like-minded friends. I travel across the city day and night, from east to west, leaving no time for anything else," once wrote Kikusha-ni. Yet she eventually decided to return home. On her way she stopped over at her teacher Sankyō's home in Mino. There she attended poetry gatherings almost every day and received lessons in tea ceremony from Sankyō's master Itō Munenaga, the chief retainer of a *hatamoto* (a high-ranking vassal of the shogun) family. When leaving Mino, she was sent off by her teacher and fellow poets, who hosted a grand farewell poetry party for her. She stopped at Kyoto, boarded a boat at Osaka, sailed across the Seto Inland Sea, and returned to her parents after five years. She kept a journal of this voyage with the title *"Taorigiku 1: hana no maki"* (A single Chrysanthemum, Chapter One: Flowers).

Kikusha-ni celebrated the New Year with her parents and settled in Chōfu. But in the following year Hyakuchabō, a *haikai* friend from Mino, called on her and suggested a journey to Kyūshū,[25] to which she agreed. According to her *"Futatabi-zue"* (Back to the Road with a Walking Stick), they extended their journey as far as Nagasaki and Kumamoto to spread the *haikai* of the Mino school, spent the New Year's holiday in Nagasaki, climbed Mt. Aso, and returned home. In the fall of the same year she headed for Mino to send off Hyakuchabō and paid a visit to her ailing teacher.

At the age of thirty-eight she went to Kyoto for the third time, to attend a ceremony commemorating the one-hundredth anniversary of the passing of Bashō. She enjoyed touring Uji, Nara, Yoshino, and Osaka. One night in Yoshino, after all the cherry blossoms fell,[26] a heavy rain struck. To escape the rain, she stayed overnight in Saigyō-an, a hut named after Saigyō, a great *waka* poet of the 12th century.[27] It was at that time that Kikusha-ni began to compose *waka* as well. Following is her first *waka*, as recorded in *"Taorigiku 3: kaze no maki"* (A Single Chrysanthemum, Chapter Three: Winds).

> Even in summer
> Mt Yoshino appears as if it were
> blanketed with cherry blossoms,[28]
> white clouds hanging over
> the green leaves on the mountain ridge

At the age of forty-one, Kikusha-ni once again left for Edo, where she visited Sakuzaemon, an artisan whose acquaintance she had previously made. Sakuzaemon made her a seven-string *koto* harp and introduced her to Kikuchi Tōgen, a retainer of the Satsuma daimyo, who would be her instructor in the instrument. After the New Year's holidays, she left Edo to start her journey west, carrying her seven-string *koto*. On her way she drew the landscapes of the fifty-three post stations on the Tōkaidō, composed poems suitable to attach to the drawings, and gave away her work as a gift at each station. One can find drafts of those works in *"Taorigiku 2: shima no maki"* (A Single Chrysanthemum, Chapter Two: Islands), drawings that combine powerful brush strokes and beautiful colors in light, gentle tones.[29]

Traveling along the Tōkaidō, Kikusha-ni arrived in Kyoto. In this old capital she socialized with court aristocrats and renowned artists, whom she engaged in tea ceremonies and gatherings for *haikai*, *waka* and music. She had the honor of having her seven-string *koto* named *Ryūsui* (flowing water) by Saionji Yoshisue, a member of a noble family and the former Great Minister of the Left.[30] To have the name carved on her instrument, she asked the expertise of Nakamura Sōtetsu, a maestro artisan of traditional arts and crafts. She then received further training in *koto* from nobleman Hiramatsu Tokiaki, the Middle Councilor,[31] known as the saint of *koto*. Her devotion pushed her to even learn the voiceless sounds required for singing with the instrument. Through these gatherings, Kikusha-ni deepened her friendship with renowned people of taste in Kyoto.[32]

In 1796 the forty-four-year-old nun left for Nagasaki again, carrying her treasured musical instrument. She continued to attend *haikai* gatherings on her way, but her main objective for this trip was to learn *kanshi*, classic Chinese verses. She took lessons in *kanshi* from a Confucian scholar in the city, who also taught her how to pronounce specific necessary sounds, such as plosives and nasals. At this time she created a unique literary style, which was to express a poetic theme twice, via *hokku* and *kanshi*, and to inscribe them calligraphically side by side. During her two-year stay in Kyūshū, Kikusha-ni devoted herself to *kanshi*, composing verses in its varied forms. She was bold enough to present her original *kanshi* even to native-speaking Chinese, such as Confucian scholar Jiang Lingzhou and painter Fei Qinghu, then residing in Tōjin-mura (Chinese village) in the suburbs of Nagasaki. She developed friendships with renowned Japanese Confucian scholars and Zen monks as well, to whom she also sent her *kanshi* verses.

In the autumn of her fifty-first year Kikusha-ni embarked upon her third trip to Kyūshū. In Beppu, a famous hot spring resort, where locals used the clear water springing from the earth for cooking, the poetess hosted an outdoor tea ceremony, simply spreading a rug on the ground, with freshly harvested tea. She wrote:

> Its poetic grace is not shallow. The cup reflects the sky where winds were blowing and clouds trailing. Fragrant winds clearly carry the color of bluish clouds, reminiscent of the evening sky reflecting the setting sun. . . .

> Traveling across the surface
> of a *Tenmoku* cup[33] are the clouds
> in the autumn sky

With her Chinese style tea cup reflecting the clouds of the Japanese sky, Kikusha-ni was deeply content, relaxed and steeped in the calm of the earth. She stayed in Beppu for about one month, and then climbed over the mountains to head for Hakata in Chikuzen province. She visited men of letters there, such as the Confucian scholar Kamei Nanmei[34] and his brother Don-ei, a Zen monk, to whom she presented her works in her unique style: *kanshi* and *hokku* written together side by side. She extended her journey to Yanagawa and Kumamoto, spending over a year in literary and musical activities.

Kikusha-ni's journey seemed never to stop. She made her fourth tour of Kyūshū at the age of fifty-three and in the following year she headed for Kyoto, her fourth trip there, where she spent over one hundred days.

She began to refrain from going too far away from her mother, devoting herself to the old widow. She instead participated in the cultural life of the nearby villages, hosting tea ceremonies at *haikai* gatherings, visiting the graves of her former in-laws, and strolling along reciting poetry, always with her precious *koto*.

Kikusha-ni, however, could never quell her desire for travel. It might have been that her *koto* named for the flowing water tempted the poetess, or perhaps her bohemian nature left her restless. It was the spring of her fifty-ninth year in 1811 when she started her fifth trip to Kyoto, leaving her eighty-year-old mother behind. The specific purpose for the trip was to attend the ceremony commemorating the five-hundred-fiftieth anniversary of the death of the Buddhist saint Shinran. Kikusha-ni took the sea route via the Seto Inland Sea to Osaka, where she sojourned briefly before proceeding to Kyoto. There she paid a visit to Hiramatsu Tokiaki, the legend of *koto* and her old teacher, to whom she presented her own drawing and poem. In the tenth month she hosted a tea ceremony at the noted temple Daitoku-ji to celebrate her soon-to-come sixtieth birthday. The lay Buddhist nun invited those with whom she had socialized over all those years, and entertained them with only the humble tea cup and her *koto*, which she had carried along in her humble travel sack.

While in Kyoto, Kikusha-ni spent days and nights with her poet friends, including nobles of the Saionji and Tokudaiji families. In the spring of the following year, she had the opportunity to present a poem to Mōri Motoyoshi, daimyo of Chōfu, her home domain, who was staying in Fushimi (near Kyoto) on his way to Edo for his alternate attendance (*sankin kōtai*).[35] From there she traveled down the river to Osaka and visited her friend Baba Eiko. The nun instructed her friend in the art of playing classical *koto*, which she had learned from Hiramatsu Tokiaki; then she gave her the beloved instrument. Kikusha-ni returned to Kyoto, where she was invited by the chief priest of Saitoku-ji for a trip to Hōryū-ji[36] in Nara; there was to be an exhibition of a Buddhist image at the temple, a ceremony held only once in thirty-three years. At Hōryū-ji, she not only had the pleasure of viewing the temple's treasures but was allowed to play an old *koto* preserved there since the eighth century. She wrote in "*Taorigiku, shigatsu no maki*" (A Single Chrysanthemum, Fourth Month): "With the blessing of the Buddha, I played and dedicated a tune to the revered Prince Shōtoku, kneeling down in front of his precious image. Indeed the ancient instrument of thousands of years preserved a noble sound. It evoked in my heart the image of the time when the saint was enshrined in the temple. I was deeply moved."

After completing this fifteen-month journey, Kikusha-ni published a record of her travels over the preceding thirty-three years in the four chapters of "*Taorigiku*" (A Single Chrysanthemum) from a renowned publisher in Kyoto. She wrote the preface herself to commemorate her sixtieth birthday.

From then on, the nun did not leave records of any long distance travels but continued socializing with her artist and poet friends. She repeatedly visited local villages and strolled in the mountains, fields, temples, and shrines, reciting poems, until her death at seventy four.

Kikusha-ni's journeys are said to extend to twenty seven thousand kilometers in total. She was perhaps the most traveled woman in the Edo period considering the distance she covered and the number of years she spent on her journeys.

Pursuit of Literary Art—A Kanshi Poetess

Hara Saihin[37] was the daughter of the Confucian scholar Hara Kosho of Akizuki, a subordinate domain of Fukuoka in Chikuzen province. Since the age of eight, she had often accompanied her father to visit his teacher Kamei Nanmei in Fukuoka, where she would socialize with Nanmei's son Shōyō and granddaughter Shōkin. Thus, the young Saihin was no stranger to the world of scholarship. At eighteen, she traveled east with her parents to see the broader world, staying in the provinces of Suō, Nagato, and Aki. In

Hiroshima, the family was welcomed by the Confucian scholar Rai Shunsui (the father of Rai San'yō) and his wife Baishi. Wherever they went, Saihin and her parents would meet like-minded people, compose poems together, and exchange cups of *sake*. Her father also took her several times to see the scholar Hirose Tansō of Bungo province, the founder of the private Kangi-en academy in Hita. The twenty-three-year-old Saihin is depicted in Tansō's memoir *Kaikyūrō-hikki* (Notes from the Tower of Nostalgia) vol.20 as follows: "The young woman has been reading since childhood, has familiarized herself with works of literature, and is gifted in composing poems. Her manners are frank and unaffected. She is not bothered by minute details nor particularly compelled to appear feminine. She enjoys drinking." Saihin was said to have traveled dressed like a man in her later years,[38] and was indeed fond of *sake* throughout her life. After this visit she and her father extended their journey to Saga and Nagasaki.

It was the first month of 1825 when Saihin left home alone for Edo to study. On her way she stopped in Fukuoka to bid farewell to her old family friends Kamei Shōyō and his daughter Shōkin. Shōyō rejoiced over her visit and entertained her with his disciples and his daughter, who had already married into another family but was called back by her father for the occasion. Shōkin expressed her thoughts in a *kanshi* which she had her father compose for her,[39] and dedicated it to Saihin as her farewell words. In it she vehemently objected to Saihin's traveling alone, advising that a woman's place was in the home.[40] But Saihin's determination never wavered.

On her way to Kyoto she visited friends of her father, from whom she sought guidance for her studies. During her yearlong stay in Kyoto, Saihin energetically composed poems at various locations near the old capital, such as Nara, Yoshino, Ama-no-hashidate, and Tango province. But when she received word of her father's illness, she hurried back home, canceling her original plan of travelling to Edo.

Saihin devoted herself to nursing her father until his death early in 1827. After mourning for six months, she left her mother in Akizuki and headed once again for Kyoto. In her inner pocket she carefully carried a seal she inherited from her father, which had originally been left for him by the late Kamei Nanmei. On the seal were carved characters that read, "a traveler who knows no borders" meaning "a free person"[41] She kept this memento close throughout her life, likely as a symbol of her pride in being a woman of free spirit. In fact, Saihin's determination was fortified by her late father's strongly supportive wishes.[42] Kosho, her father, had two sons, one older than Saihin and the other younger, but both were delicate in nature. The father took his daughter, not his sons, travelling from the time she was young; he saw to it that she received lessons from the local scholars, probably because he had recognized her talent early. The daughter satisfied his expectations and soon was reciting Chinese classical poems alongside Confucian scholars. For her part, Saihin probably felt a strong responsibility to find acclaim as a scholar-poet so that her father's honor might be vindicated, as he had been expelled from his professorship at the domain school for political reasons.[43] Equally importantly, perhaps, she intended to financially support the household, as well. In a letter to a friend, recorded in "*Tōyū nikki*" (A Study Tour to the East), Saihin composed a poem, saying that there was something she had vowed to accomplish and that she could not return home without having made her name.

She bade farewell to her brothers at Iwakuma in Buzen province, where the two men resided for health reasons, running a private academy. Now Saihin's solitary journey began. From Akamagaseki she took a boat to Miyajima.[44] She had once visited the island with her parents, and now it surely invoked nostalgia for that lost time. Disembarking at Hatsukaichi, she visited old friends of her late father's in Hiroshima and Fuchū, where she composed and recited *kanshi* and exchanged cups of *sake*. She was also welcomed by Rai San'yō's uncle Kyōhei and mother Baishi, who hosted a moon viewing party for her. Kyōhei kindly wrote reference letters for her, as a result of which Saihin was received warmly everywhere she visited in the region. At times she earned her travel fund working as a scribe or lecturing on *kanshi* for wealthy families here and there, and developed friendships with them while continuing her studies. Certainly, she was helped by the letters of reference that Kyōhei and other friends of her father wrote for her. Yet she would not have been so widely welcomed had it not been for her talents and her genial personality.

She celebrated the New Year at Confucian scholar Mano Chikudō's residence at Kunai in Bitchū province. After offering New Year's prayers at Kibi Shrine, Saihin called on Fujii Takanao, the renowned National studies[45] scholar, at his official residence on the shrine grounds. In the middle of the first month she arrived in Okayama and ten days later reached Akō, where she stayed with Oda Bankoku for about two months. Her journal indicates that she taught calligraphy and lectured on poetry at the request of local people. She left Akō at the end of the third month and visited people of letters in Tatsuno, Himeji, and Akashi. Her travels continued, repeatedly bringing her the joy and sadness that accompanied encountering and parting with people. She arrived in Hyōgo in the middle of the fourth month.

Her journal "*Tōyū nikki*" (A Study Tour to the East) records her eleven-month journey. It begins in the sixth month, as she leaves her hometown of Akizuki, and ends after she reaches Hyōgo. It consists of a large number of *kanshi* composed during her trip, and prose descriptions of various activities.

After Hyōgo, she continued to travel east to Kyoto, where she met with Rai San'yō and Yanagawa Seigan, the poet from Ōgaki in Mino province.[46] She asked for their critique of her *kanshi* drafts and received praise and encouragement. Since Saihin was going to continue her travel further east to Edo, Seigan volunteered to write introduction letters addressed to prominent people she might meet along the way.

Travel was synonymous with learning for Saihin. On her way to Edo, Saihin continued to socialize with scholars, poets, and artists, always composing poems and exchanging cups of *sake* with them. Her devotion to her training in poetry continued throughout her life.

Saihin arrived in Edo in the winter of 1828. She was thirty-one. Through the good offices of Matsuzaki Kōdō, a Confucian scholar, she settled in the temple Shōnen-ji at Asakusa. She actively continued her intellectual pursuits, developing connections with clansmen from various domains stationed in Edo, renowned Confucian scholars, and poets such as Ōnuma Chinzan. Saihin would be invited to daimyo mansions, as well, to lecture on Chinese classics, such as *Shu Jing* and *Shi Jing*. Diary entries, though sketchy, are included in the manuscript of her *kanshi* collection "*Yūkirō-shikō*" (Poems of the Shining Tower) which records her activities in the city in the first month through the fourth month of 1831 and the first month of 1842. Among the extremely brief descriptions, perhaps too short to call a diary, are scattered numbers and words such as those meaning "spinning," "spinning all day," and "workshop labor." Apparently the scholar-poet spent considerable time spinning and sewing to support herself in addition to her normal activities as a scribe and lecturer. But obviously she also devoted many hours to the composition of *kanshi*.

Saihin came to be on familiar terms with her landlords: the chief priest of Shōnen-ji and his wife. She would keep him company drinking, and accompany his wife on various day trips. Her diary includes a record of their outing to Ueno to enjoy its famous cherry blossoms. When the wife was sick in bed, Saihin would nurse her, chatting with her and sipping her favorite drink at her bedside. She would call on *kanshi* poets and Confucian scholars, and in return they would often visit her at the temple. In either case *sake* was ubiquitous, accompanied by spirited poetic exchanges. She often suffered foot pains, probably gout from excessive drinking.

There is record of her frequent visits to the Edo residence of Kurume domain, perhaps due to her official status as an adopted daughter of Toyoshima Sazen, a Kurume clansman. It was a formality she had undergone to obtain permission to leave her home province. Among the samurai houses she frequented in Edo were the residences of Tsu, Aizu, and Yonezawa domains. On her way home from such visits she would sometimes run into her friends and be invited to their homes, where she would enjoy the usual poetic exchanges and consumption of *sake*, occasionally ending up staying with them overnight. Her connections included a *kanshi* poetess in the same neighborhood, named Shinoda Unpō,[47] whom Saihin would often visit. Koga Tōan, a scholar of the *bakufu*'s official school Shōheikō, and his brother Kokudō, a retainer of Saga domain, were also among her intellectual friends, whom she would ask to critique her poems.

Saihin's days were thus largely occupied with the composition of *kanshi*, lecturing on Chinese classics, sightseeing, and poetic gatherings, all of which she carried out while lodging at the homes of her friends and acquaintances in and near Edo. Indeed she frequently traveled the areas surrounding Edo in the 1840s. Although she did not leave journals at the time, her *kanshi* poems diligently trace her footsteps. Destinations included the Bōsō Peninsula, Musashi, Kōzuke, Shimotsuke, Nikkō, and other towns and villages of the Kantō region. This series of frequent short trips ended after she returned from her second visit to Bōsō in 1847.

When she left for Bōsō for the second time, the poetess was fifty years old and had already lived in Edo for eighteen years. One autumn day she left Edo by boat and landed on Kisarazu. Then in Futtsu and Katsuyama she sought a few nights' lodgings at the homes of village headmen, scholars, and physicians, who were all her acquaintances. She eventually arrived at Yamukaimura and sojourned at Suzuki Shōtō's place. Shōtō was a disciple of the scholar Yanagawa Seigan; Seigan had also traveled the Bōsō Peninsula with his wife Kōran six years earlier. Shōtō apparently welcomed Saihin enthusiastically. He gave the Sino-Japanese pen name Sairan, after both Kōran and Saihin, to his second daughter Sawa, who was born the year after Saihin arrived. Sairan learned *kanshi* from her father and later assisted him in teaching his female disciples at Nanamagari-ginsha (an association of *kanshi* poets) and his private Kōyū-juku academy. Her pupils included Mita Ranyū, Suzuki Shikō, and Iwata Shōhin, who all became accomplished *kanshi* poetesses in the Meiji era which followed.

Saihin spent the New Year's holidays at the Yukues, the family of a village headman in Shirahama on the peninsula. It was indeed a relaxing vacation for her, reciting poems with those who would gather at the house by the shore. Having met and parted with many people, she now traveled north along Kujūkuri-hama beach on the east coast of the peninsula and arrived at the house of Saitō Goseidō (Kimikazu),[48] the strongman overseeing all the fishing villages of the region. Here she concludes her "*Tōyū mansō*" (Poems from the Eastern Tour) a collection of *kanshi* which depicts her journey through the Bōsō Peninsula. She probably went back to Edo before the summer, trying to avoid traveling in the sweltering heat. In addition to "*Tōyū mansō*," Saihin left a list of the names of people and villages on a few sheets of paper, presumably related to the lodgings she took up during her journey.

Saihin's decision to visit the peninsula again for the first time in eighteen years was perhaps inspired by Yanagawa Seigan and his wife Kōran, who had traveled Bōsō six years before. During her first trip there she must have felt quite lonely and challenged in many ways since it had been only two years since she had come to Edo and was not familiar with the region. But her second trip was different, as she was warmly welcomed by the people wherever she went, thanks to her own reputation as a scholar-poet in Edo. The reference letters Seigan wrote for her also helped. She now saw with her own eyes the places of scenic beauty that Seigan and Kōran had depicted in their collections of *kanshi*. It must have been one of her most fruitful journeys.

Journey to a Late Husband's Home

Saisho Atsuko, the wife of Saisho Atsuyuki, a retainer of the Satsuma daimyo, was widowed eight years after they married. Being left alone with her only daughter Tokuko, Atsuko found herself totally lost when he died but soon pulled herself together and found her path of duty; she would move to Kagoshima, Atsuyuki's home, to look after her mother-in-law and raise her two stepdaughters, whom her late husband had fathered in his earlier marriage.

In the fourth month of 1853, soon after the first anniversary of his death, Atsuko visited Atsuyuki's grave at Tōfuku-ji, bade farewell to close friends and acquaintances and left for the faraway province. She left the home where she had spent her almost three decades on Earth. People around her objected to her decision to go to the "land so far as to border with China"[49] but could not influence the firmly determined Atsuko.

She sailed down the Takase River and changed to another boat at Fushimi to descend the Yodo River through the night, when a storm hit, leaving even courageous Atsuko disoriented. After landing at Naniwa, she was accompanied by some clansmen of Satsuma but was unable to exchange friendly conversation with them at that time. A rather melancholic overland journey continued. When they were passing the scenic inlet of Suma, Atsuko was so unwell that she did not even feel like stepping out of her palanquin to enjoy the view. But her melancholy apparently lifted before long, and she visited a few famous shrines in the Akashi area. By the time the party reached Itozaki in Bingo province she was ready to appreciate the landscape that was "not inferior to the coastline of Suma and Akashi." Atsuko was also moved by the rain clouds covering the peak of an offshore mountain island, a view not found in Kyoto. She writes, "I would not have been able to admire such a novel landscape had it not been for this journey. It was indeed worthwhile

leaving home." Her homesickness for Kyoto gradually faded while she continued to accumulate various travel experiences. The following *waka* depicts
her joy at drinking water from a spring after crossing a bumpy mountain road
in the heat of summer:

> The clear spring water
> deep in the hills, cupped in my hands
> with its cool purity,
> makes one forget for a moment
> even one's beloved home

Sea travel was not without frightening moments, either, but Atsuko forgot
them all when she visited Itsukushima[50] on 5.13. The view of the shrine's
palatial buildings and its surroundings indeed equaled its reputation as one of
the top three sights in the country and was even superior to the drawings she
had seen of it. It so deeply captivated her that she was quite rueful when the
return boat quickly sailed away from the island. On that day the party still had
a long way to go before reaching their night's lodging, therefore they hurried
along the mountain roads through the dark. Atsuko fell asleep in her palanquin, probably fatigued from her daytime excitement about the magnificent
beauty of Itsukushima Shrine. Still in slumber, she was oblivious to their arrival at the inn. She wrote with embarrassment, "It was so careless of me and
regrettable for not having been better composed."

The party arrived in Kyūshū on 5.22. The high quality of the water at the
Yamaga hot springs pleased Atsuko tremendously. Her personal knowledge
of hot springs had been so far limited to Arima near Kyoto, and she was
disappointed that her itinerary could not allow her a longer stay in Yamaga.
When they entered the castle town of Kagoshima on 6.1, her journey of
nearly thirty days came to an end. It is recorded in her diary "*Kokoro zukushi*"
(Thoughts on the Journey).

Visiting a Late Husband's Grave

Hidaka Tsutako at last found the opportunity to visit her late husband's grave
when she was fifty-three in 1867. Hidaka Jisui had been a professor at the domain school Meirindō of Takanabe in Hyūga province, but died twenty years
earlier at the age of thirty-nine while studying under a Confucian scholar in
Osaka. He was buried at Jōkoku-ji in Tennōji (central Osaka). Since that day
Tsutako devoted herself to raising their three sons but never forgot even for a
day her wish to visit Jisui's grave there. Her eldest son followed his father's
path, becoming assistant professor at Meirindō and going for further training

in Edo and Osaka. Finishing his studies, he summoned his mother to Osaka so that she might realize her long-cherished wish.

Tsutako left Takanabe on horseback, her daughters-in-law and grandchildren gathering to send her off.[51] At various stops along the way, she was offered going-away gifts by well-wishers and exchanged cups of *sake* with them. On the first day of the second month, she left Mimitsu by boat. By the time it was passing the coast of Kamae (in northeastern Kyūshū), two other women on board had taken badly seasick, yet Tsutako was fine and busy composing poetry. Sailing before the wind the following day, the boat swiftly passed Moji, Kaminoseki, and Hiroshima. The wind dropped off near Mihara, where they anchored. Later, the party visited Konpira Shrine in Shikoku, the boat anchoring overnight at Tadotsu. At the shrine Tsutako dedicated *sake* and offered prayers for the safety of the rest of their voyage.

On the Sea of Harima, known for its rough waters, people on shipboard performed ceremonial prayers and offered *sake* to appease the gods. Their prayers were apparently heard, and the boat proceeded smoothly with a favorable wind. Awaji Island was "too beautiful for words," according to Tsutako, who composed only a *waka* to describe its beauty. Landing at Minato in Hyōgo, Tsutako visited Ikuta Shrine with a boatman as her guide. The shrine was a tourist attraction; tradition had it that it was where renowned warrior Kajiwara Kagesue fought with a twig of plum in his quiver in the Genji-Heike War, a famous scene often adapted into *nō* drama and *bunraku* puppet plays, and depicted in various art works. Inspired by the old story, Tsutako wrote a *waka* for a withered plum tree in the district. She continued her tour to the grave of Kusunoki Masashige, another historical figure, at Minatogawa Shrine. She strolled around the neighborhood, remembering the warrior, who had killed himself at the Battle of Minatogawa after being defeated by his enemy. In the following *waka* she praised the war hero from the Northern and Southern Dynasties period, who rose in arms at the order of Emperor Godaigo:

> The Minato River—
> though your flow may dry,
> the fragrant name
> of the honorable warrior
> remains in our hearts

Tsutako, having safely completed the nine-day voyage, finally visited her late husband's grave. Although together with her eldest son, her loneliness was profound.

> Coming to see you,
> I ask you of various

matters in Naniwa,
but there comes no response
from the moss-green grave

All she could do was to pray at the gravesite with a thousand emotions surging in her breast, wrote Tsutako in her diary "*Kono hana nikki*" (Plum Blossom Diary).

Visiting the Natal Home

In the third month of 1822, Morimoto Tsuzuko and her husband Mayumi, a village headman, traveled together to visit Tsuzuko's mother, who had been longing to see her daughter for some time. It was a journey from Shimadamura of Iida in landlocked Shinano province to Hamamatsu, a town on the Pacific Coast. Before their departure, Tsuzuko's father came to the village, crossing the mountains to accompany them on their journey.

The three set off with two male attendants assisting as porters. Mayumi was a busy man, who, in addition to his responsibilities as village master, was officially assigned to contribute to the finances of the Hori family, daimyo of Iida. Nevertheless, he offered to accompany his wife on her visit.

They crossed the Tenryū River, overnighting at a village nearby, and reached the Ogawaji Pass. There, overlooking distant Shimadamura, they parted with the people who had accompanied them so far to send them off. Clad in straw rain capes, they traversed the passes under a drizzling sky, finally arriving at the village of Kizawa. They looked for accommodation there but could not find an appropriate place with vacant rooms, eventually settling for lodging at a shabby inn. The next day the party crossed over the steep Aokuzure Pass and rested at a tea stall at the border between Shinano and Tōtōmi. They sampled the local specialty, *konnyaku* (rectangular jellies made from devil's-tongue) which had white sesame seed paste spread on one side and *miso* on the other, representing the snow of Shinano and the red soil of Tōtōmi respectively. After visiting Akiha Shrine, they sailed down the Tenryū River to Ōtanimura and called at the house of Uchiyama Matatsu, the couple's mentor in *waka*, who had been living there in seclusion. There, they were told that their *waka* master had passed away a year prior. That night they lodged at the house and recounted their memories of the master all night long. Leaving, they called on Takabayashi Michiakira, another *waka* master, but again they could not see him, as he happened to not be at home that day. Later the same day, the party arrived at Tsuzuko's parents' house.

From that day on, family friends and close acquaintances visited one after another, and parties were frequently thrown for them. The couple enjoyed their vacation, visiting temples and shrines with their clan and close friends, boating on the river, and collecting seashells on the beach. One day Tsuzuko, who was thirty-three and childless, was guided to Harameishi Shrine (the god of pregnancy), where she bowed holding a stone and offered a *waka* to the god:

> Even a simple stone
> may become pregnant
> by god's grace,
> How I pray to be blessed with
> a child, a beautiful shining jade

The couple was overjoyed by the birth of a son the following year.

During their sojourn they sometimes received visits from Takabayashi Michiakira, the *waka* poet mentioned above, who offered them lectures on the *Kokinshū*.[52] Tsuzuko herself would host *waka* meetings with her poet friends as well. She also had the opportunity one day to go to see a daimyo procession crossing the Tenryū River, a pageant never seen in their village in Iida. As the day of their departure approached, people came, some from faraway places, to say goodbye. On their return trip, the couple's retinue followed the Tōkaidō to Toyokawa-inari Shrine, and spent the night in Akasaka.[53] Passing Fujikawa they travelled through Okazaki, where Tsuzuko was somewhat concerned and withdrawn, for she had read that in Okazaki there were many flirting harlots. Fortunately, they encountered no such creature. They lodged in Chiryū, visited Atsuta Shrine, and the city of Nagoya. Leaving Nagoya on 5.5, the party traveled on foot, sometimes hiring palanquin services as needed, and reached Nakatsugawa (in present-day Gifu prefecture) on the Nakasendō. They crossed the Jikkoku Pass on the border between Mino and Shinano, and two kilometers later climbed the Magome Pass. They slept that night in a village called Hirosemura. The following day they climbed the high, painful Kiso Pass, where not even a single ray of light could filter through the trees. Descending through the pass, they re-entered the territory of their local Hori clan. Climbing over Mt. Kazakoshi, they reached Sunaharai, where the party was met by well-wishers who had come to greet them. They exchanged cups of *sake* to celebrate their safe return and went home singing.

Both Mayumi and Tsuzuko wrote accounts of this two-month trip home in their respective travel diaries. Tsuzuko titled hers "*Yumeji nikki*" (Traveling the Land of Dreams).

Convalescence at Hot Springs

Tsuzuko wrote another travel diary in 1836, fourteen years after the *Yumeji nikki*, when she was forty-seven years old. It is an account of a trip for a hot spring cure entitled "*Suwa nikki*" (Suwa Diary).

On a cold day in the eleventh month she left for the treatment of an injury suffered by her only son Masahisa. Masahisa was the child born the year after she had offered prayers at Harameishi Shrine. The couple treasured this child, to whom Tsuzuko had given birth in her mid-thirties. They were raising him with great care, but one day he wrenched his ankle and was badly injured. His pained parents wondered what to do, when they heard about a renowned doctor in the field, who served the Suwa family of Takashima domain. They decided right away to take their son to the doctor and left for Shimo-Suwa accompanied by a relative named Fukuzumi.

At their lodging on the second day in Ōtagiri, Tsuzuko was horrified to hear that a heavy rain that summer had caused a river to flood the area, killing several people. But when they reached a hilly, rustic area in the heart of the mountains, they caught a glimpse of the surface of Lake Suwa reflecting the soaring summit of Mt. Fuji. The view reminded Tsuzuko of the inlet depicted in a famous *waka* by the ancient poet Yamabe no Akahito.[54] The beauty of the place apparently inspired her son as well, who said he would love to draw the landscape.

On the fifth day they arrived at their destination and settled in an inn called Takeya, which they had chosen for their sojourn. That night a minor incident occurred at the inn. A guest found all his clothes and belongings gone when he came out of the bath. He yelled his heart out, "Thieves, thieves!" Agitated by the great commotion, the people in the house all came out to search every corner of the establishment as well as the streets nearby. The search continued until dawn, when at last the thief was caught. Naturally, Tsuzuko spent the entire night sleepless.

They spent the first few days visiting the renowned doctor for treatment, praying at Kami-Suwa Shrine, and with a visit to the Jizō Bodhisattva at Furusawa hot springs, the deity to which Tsuzuko had once offered prayers for the recovery of her husband's injured leg. Presently Mayumi departed to return to Iida, while Tsuzuko and their son, along with the relative who accompanied them, stayed for further treatment for Masahisa. From the house next to their lodging came loud noises that made Tsuzuko uncomfortable; apparently men and women were drinking together, singing and flirting. There were stormy days and snowy days, when the mother and the son were both homesick for Iida.

One day a messenger came from home, delivering a poem from her husband. She opened it hurriedly and found the following *waka*:

> Chirping plovers—
> are they longing for their wives
> I wonder,
> just like I long for my wife
> in the cold bed on a stormy night

Tsuzuko immediately composed a reply poem and handed it to the messenger.

> The sea of Suwa—
> winds blow through the withered reeds
> in the clear, crisp air,
> Here, too, is a plover
> chirping longingly

Their *sōmonka* (love poems)[55] demonstrate the strong bond between the middle-aged couple, who could not but express their loneliness for each other while apart, even if only for a limited number of days.

Completing their fifteen-day sojourn at the hot springs, the party of three left Suwa for the return trip.

In Tsuzuko's two travel diaries we find various warm relationships among the members of this village master's large family: conjugal love, the parent-child bond, affectionate feelings for relatives, propriety and loyalty between mentor and student, as well as between a family and their servants.

In addition to Tsuzuko, often housewives who went to hot spring resorts for recuperation would express similar sentiments in their journals; their minds were occupied with the thought of their families left behind and wishes for a return to their warm embrace.

Ikeda Kiyoi, the wife of a retainer of the Shōnai daimyo in Dewa province, went in the eighth month of 1841 to the Atsumi spa for convalescence from illness and in hopes of improving the poor condition of her legs. Though the resort was not far from her home, her mind was constantly with her family, especially her two young sons and her father-in-law Gensai, a scholar who was visually impaired.[56] Seeing the colorfully tinted leaves, Kiyoi wished Gensai had been able to admire the autumn beauty with her. She took up a brush, drew the leaves, and enclosed the drawing in her letter home. In her diary she wrote about the harvest moon:

> The moon rises in the clear sky and brightly illuminates the treetops, as if telling me to count the number of falling leaves. Indeed, had it not been for a village in a mountain valley like this, would I ever have the opportunity to see such an attractive moon? Appreciating the splendid view all by myself, I cannot help but feel for my father-in-law and the young boys. I wonder how they are passing their days.

Thus Kiyoi's mind strayed back to her home, even while deeply appreciating the supreme beauty of nature and the serenity of the moon. Her diary continues:

I composed this poem thinking of how my father-in-law and the young ones were waiting for me at home.

> Is it pine crickets
> chirping under the dewed leaves,
> like my loved ones
> waiting for me and urging my
> early return?

Though she had not thoroughly recuperated from her illness, Kiyoi hurried home after staying at the resort for about twenty days. Home in Tsuruoka, she resumed the daily routine that included house chores, child care, supervising the servants, and more than anything else, assisting her scholarly father-in-law in his writing. Kiyoi herself was of weak constitution, and perhaps her heavy responsibilities were overwhelming; she ended her short life at the age of thirty-one, a year after her stay at the Atsumi hot springs. She was survived by the men of the family: her husband, father-in-law and two sons.

Journey for Petition

Kurosawa Toki of Suzukōyamura in Hitachi province (northeast of Edo) began a journey to Kyoto in the second month of 1859, leaving her aging mother at home. She had been enraged by the *bakufu* order of domiciliary confinement for Tokugawa Nariaki, the former Mito daimyo, during the Purge of the Ansei Era (*Ansei no taigoku*).[57] She composed a *chōka* (long poem)[58] to present to the Imperial Court, in which she complained of the *bakufu*'s misrule, contended the innocence of Nariaki, and petitioned for his release. Believing the white comet that appeared at the time to be a revelation of the beginning of a turbulent period, she decided to travel to Kyoto, wishing to right this injustice, though she was already fifty-four years old.

To avoid the *bakufu*'s inspections of travelers, she commenced her clandestine journey without an official travel permit. All she had was money borrowed against her small savings and household effects.

Her *waka* disciples accompanied her as far as Kasama, where they parted and she took her first night's lodging. The following day she was asked by a stranger to escort a boy to Shimodate. Toki was happy to have a travel companion and agreed to take him there. In Shimodate she availed herself of one night's accommodation at the home of an acquaintance, where she ended up staying another full day due to the rain.

When she passed the town of Oyama, Toki was caught up to by a Shinto priest from her village, who had departed three days after her, and received the news that he would accompany her to Kyoto. Toki was greatly heartened.

At their lodging in Sano, they came across three male travelers discussing politics all through the night, but Toki and the priest pretended to be uninterested. The following morning they hired a horse to hurry to Ashikaga, then walked to Kiryū and stayed at an inn, which Toki had often used while making rounds as a peddler years before. They continued their journey alternately on foot and horseback. Fatigued by the priest's rapid pace over the hilly roads in cold winter, Toki rested at the Sawatari hot springs, visited the home of an acquaintance nearby, and parted with the priest to refresh herself for a while. In Kusatsu she stayed for about three days at an inn run by another acquaintance of hers, to whose grandchild she had previously taught penmanship. Coincidentally, a local relative was also travelling to the vicinity of Zenkō-ji, so they decided to travel together.

The long Shibu Pass (approximately 30 kilometers) at the border was the most perilous part of her journey. Clinging to her cane and heavily perspiring, she climbed, fighting her way through more than a meter of snow. Below her was a ravine one thousand feet deep, and with one false step they could have fallen to its bottom. She endured all those hardships for "my lord, and for the entire country," overcoming every frozen step on the snowy mountain path. They finally began descending, but there still were obstacles, such as the big ponds said to be inhabited by huge serpents. They walked past the ponds, frantically gasping and panting, half buried in the snow. Toki's face was hurting from frostbite and her legs were bone tired when they found their way to the Shibu hot springs at last.

On the day after their arrival at the hot springs, Toki was too tired to walk even one step further. She let her companion leave for the temple alone, while recuperating in the bath. The next day at Zenkō-ji, she observed a crowd of men and women of all ages "swarming like armies of ants." It happened to be the annual exhibition of the temple's principal image of Amida-nyorai. She then visited Togakushi Shrine[59] with an elderly woman she had met at the inn, who had asked Toki to accompany her there. Toki requested special prayers at the shrine for "peace and security for the country, as well as safety of my journey to achieve a great deed for our lord's continued luck in arms." Returning to Zenkō-ji, Toki prayed one more time and resumed her journey. She was now with some pilgrims whom she had met at Zenkō-ji. They walked together chatting as far as Kuwaharajuku,[60] where she sought accommodation for the night.

Resting under the eaves of a stranger's house, she told the mistress that she was traveling for training in *waka*. The woman of the house offered her one night's accommodation, since "you are on a journey for training." She then began recounting to Toki her story that her husband had left their home for twelve years for training in swordsmanship, and that for all those years she had raised their three daughters by herself, overcoming various obstacles. Toki felt compassion for her, for she herself had raised two daughters while peddling and teaching children at the temple school after her husband had died. They spoke at length, for "women understand each other's hardships, wherever they may live or come from." Later, the man of the house returned home and joined their conversation. The three stayed up all night talking about difficulties in journeys and in the training they had undertaken. The next day the husband, clad in travel attire, kindly offered to show Toki the way to Mt. Ubasute (also called Obasute), a spot of interest to *waka* poets. Though she was in a hurry, Toki did not want the couple to suspect the real purpose of her travel; she therefore spent the whole day strolling about the mountain. An elderly woman at the Kannon temple asked Toki for a *waka*, and Toki obliged her. She wrote more poems on *tanzaku* (strips of fancy paper) to give away to other tourists.

From Shiojiri she took a detour called "the route for women and priests," instead of the Ina-kaidō, passed over long hilly roads and the Ōhira Pass, and found lodging at a local village. Presently she had new travel companions: a couple and their daughter, who were traveling dancers. Along the way the father recounted old war stories of both China and Japan, extending his topics to current political issues, while bad-mouthing Tokugawa Nariaki. He criticized the former Mito daimyo, repeating "Edo and Kyoto would be in chaos if the retired lord of Mito had not been ordered into indefinite confinement." Toki's heart was boiling with anger hearing this talk. She secretly told herself, "Chief Minister Ii must have schemed to trap our lord (Nariaki) for house arrest, spreading vicious rumor. How could I not take my revenge on that tyrant traitor?" With a combative spirit, she parted with the family and hurried to Kyoto. The father's stories indicate an aspect of the collective sentiment of the Edo residents at the time.

She passed Fuwa-no-seki, one of the three strictest *sekisho*[61] in ancient times,[62] traveled the Minoji road through the Jūsan Pass alone, and then slept on a bed of grass at Sekigahara. At the next stop she entered a false name in the guest register at the inn, which was under strict surveillance. On the day she offered prayers at Ishiyama-dera, Toki had difficulty finding an inn to check into alone. She then unsuccessfully tried to find a companion at Miidera to stay at Ōtsu. In the end, she walked in the rain all the way to an inn in Karasuma, Kyoto, which regularly catered to the retainers of Mito.

Toki's travel diary "*Jōkyō nikki*" (Journey to Kyoto) depicts her journey of nearly fifty days and demonstrates her fierce determination to accomplish the difficult mission, risking her life for "the sake of the country." For this reason, her travel diary is different in nature than those written by many other women.

COMPULSORY TRAVEL

Overview

Naturally travel was not always voluntary. Various circumstances obliged people to travel, and going into service was one such cause. Women of letters were sometimes summoned by their daimyo to serve as governess for his family, resident in Edo.

Inoue Tsū-jo of Marugame in Sanuki province was summoned at the age of twenty-two to serve Yōsei-in,[63] the mother of the domain lord, as her personal lecturer and literary assistant. She left two travel diaries as record of her official duties; one was "*Tōkai kikō*" (Travel along the Eastern Sea) about her journey to Edo, and the other "*Kika nikki*" (A Homeward Journey), an account of her trip home to Marugame at the age of thirty after resigning from her position upon the death of Yōsei-in. She also wrote a private journal during her homecoming journey, when she was more relaxed, with plenty of time to enjoy the scenic beauty and visit with people she encountered on her way.

Yashiro Nokawa, the adoptive mother of the administrator of Matsuyama domain, Shōnai, served as a lady-in-waiting for Matsudaira Sadanobu of the *bakufu*'s Council of Elders. When her master retired, Nokawa, then over fifty, resigned, too, and returned to Matsuyama. She wrote an account of the trip, entitled "*Tabiji no tsuyu*" (The Dew on the Roads), which includes forty-one *waka* verses that she composed on her way home. The diary indicates that Nokawa enjoyed the journey, though its purpose was not necessarily recreation.

Women also traveled not for their own official duties but as a result of their husbands' or sons' newly assigned posts. In the case of daimyo transfer from one fief to another, all the retainers and their families had to move, too.

Some women traveled for arranged marriages, leaving home for faraway lands.

During those journeys, despite their compulsory nature, these women had the freedom to enjoy their experiences, appreciating the scenic beauty, composing poems, purchasing local specialties, and so on. But those who were involved in the Boshin War, which broke out during the turbulent transitional era from the Tokugawa reign to Meiji, had no such room to savor their journeys. Instead, they had to flee from one place to another with children and the aged in tow, while at the same time avoiding the flames of war, and fighting against all sorts of obstacles to survive another day.

Summoned for Educational Service

Having moved to her late husband's home in Kagoshima, Saisho Atsuko began living with a large family of about ten, including her own daughter

Tokuko, her mother-in-law, two stepdaughters and her husband's younger brother. She served her family well, especially her mother-in-law, who was not an easy person to please. Some anecdotes tell of Atsuko's exemplary behavior; one day her mother-in-law asked her to compose a *waka* with the title "a harridan," saying that Atsuko, an accomplished poet, should honestly depict in it the hardship she had in serving her mother-in-law, whom some people might call a harridan. Atsuko smiled and recited:

> Not knowing the heart
> of my mother-in-law, kinder
> than that of the Buddha,
> people seem to call her
> a harridan, why I wonder—

The elder woman, being deeply gratified by Atsuko's poem, reportedly treated her with abundant affection from that point on. Atsuko in fact earned an impeccable reputation among people for her talent, correct conduct, chastity, filial piety and benevolent behavior towards people; which was well documented, including pertinent anecdotes by Satsuma clansmen Takasaki Masakaze and Yatsuda Tomonori, who were also *waka* poets in the Keien style. Her reputation reached the daimyo Shimazu Nariakira, who hired her as a guardian for his sixth son Tetsumaru shortly after his birth. Unfortunately, however, Nariakira and Tetsumaru died in quick succession. Atsuko was said to have considered following them in death, but desisted from doing so, so as not to leave her mother-in-law alone, composing the following *waka*, according to *Saisho Atsuko toji* (Saisho Atsuko, the matron) edited by Yashiro Kumatarō:

> Had I no obligations
> to my beloved mother-in-law,
> how I would want
> to throw myself, grief-stricken,
> into this river of tears before me

In 1863, when she was thirty-nine years old, Atsuko was appointed senior lady-in-waiting for Sadahime, the adoptive daughter of Shimazu Hisamitsu (Nariakira's younger brother), guardian of the then-daimyo Tadayoshi. Sadahime was going to marry a court noble, and Atsuko would travel with her to Kyoto.

The departure date had been scheduled for the eighth month but was delayed due to a sequence of grave incidents. The previous year, retainers of Satsuma domain had killed and injured British merchants who had dared to cross on horseback the procession of their daimyo Hisamitsu at Namamugi (northeastern Yokohama) on the Tōkaidō. Negotiations for reparations had dragged on, and in the seventh month the British fleet had fired their cannons in Kagoshima Bay, starting the Satsuma-Britain War. The war had forced Sadahime and her entourage to evacuate into the mountains.

On 11.8 the party at last commenced its journey, sent off by many people, and traveled along the Izumi road. At every village at which they stopped on their way, children performed their local dances and songs to celebrate Sadahime's departure. On the twelfth, they crossed the border at the checkpoint of Komenotsu and entered Higo province. It rained all day. Atsuko, who was in her palanquin, felt guilty, thinking of the attendants and palanquin bearers who were all soaked.

> Hiding behind
> the wings of my revered lord
> of a thousand years,
> do I travel comfortably, oblivious
> to autumn rains and cold snow

Crossing over many passes and steep hills covered with the first snow of the season, the party traveled north along the Satsuma-kaidō via the Hinaku hot springs and Yatsushiro. They arrived in Kumamoto on the sixteenth, and there they changed to the road for Tsurusaki in Bungo province. Braving the snowy Bungo-kaidō, they arrived at Tsurusaki on the twenty-first. There, the women were able to take time for ablution, fixing hairdos and carefully polishing teeth, to prepare for the sea voyage that was to begin the next day. On the twenty-sixth they left the port of Saganoseki in a large boat named the *Kokuryūmaru*. It rolled and pitched violently in the fierce winds on the Sea of Suō. Once landed at Murotsu in Harima province on the eighteenth, the passengers gave a great sigh of relief and rejoiced at their communal survival. In Himeji, the bride's party was greeted by officials from the Kyoto mansion of Satsuma domain, who guided them to renowned spots such as Suma, Akashi, Ikuta, and Sumiyoshi on their way to the imperial capital. They arrived in the capital on 12.11 and settled in the Satsuma residence at Nishiki-kōji in central Kyoto. Atsuko's diary of the journey of over thirty days is entitled "*Matsu no sakae*" (Prosperity of a Pine Tree), celebrating the bright future of Sadahime.

Returning from Service

Okada Itsu, the wife of the chief priest of Katano Shrine in Kawachi (eastern Osaka), had once served in her youth a court aristocrat named Keiko, the daughter of the Great Minister of the Right. When Keiko wedded the Matsumae daimyo, Itsu accompanied her travel all the way north to Matsumae in Hokkaidō.[64] Keiko gave birth to a child there, who died young, and she herself passed away soon after. Itsu resigned and left the town, where she had spent the previous seven years, in the eighth month of 1777.

Her return trip to Kyoto was as part of a small party of three women, unlike the grand bridal procession with which she had traveled to Matsumae. On 8.9, they sailed to a town on the Tsugaru Peninsula at the northern tip of Honshū,[65] and on the eleventh, spent the night in Aomori. Her diary records the prosperity of the city. Aomori embraced the largest port in Tsugaru domain as well as many smaller towns, stretching four kilometers with three thousand houses including eight hundred fishermen's families. Stopping over at several towns, they arrived in Morioka, the castle town of the Nanbu clan. There, too, Itsu and her companions walked about and were amazed at the thriving community. She wrote, "The appearance of the houses is not inferior to those in the capital." They continued their journey south, spending nights in several post-station towns along the way, including Hanamaki and Sendai. They crossed the Natori River, spent nights at Kurosawa and Shiraishi, then arrived in Fukushima on the twenty-sixth of the month. There, one of her companions fell ill, and the party ended up staying for eight days until her recovery.

The three women were finally able to leave Fukushima on 9.5. At Shirakawa *sekisho*, Itsu composed a *waka* expressing the loneliness of the journey:

> Autumn winds—
> tonight they pierce the forlorn figures
> standing at Shirakawa *sekisho*,
> Nobody knows (as "Shirakawa" suggests)[66]
> where they might be lodging tomorrow

On the ninth day of the ninth month, the day of the chrysanthemum festival, the women searched their travel sacks and changed to outfits suited to the season before leaving the inn. After passing Shirasaka, they arrived in Shimotsuke province. There, Itsu asked a village boy where she could find the "clear water on the roadside," a historical spot remembered in its association with the poem by Saigyō,[67] but the boy did not know. She continued to walk along the road with her companions, humming her disappointment, "Even a slight shadow of the clear stream is not to be seen."

Approaching Edo, they stopped over at Nabekake and Sakuyama, but then the party was compelled to wait one full day at Kitsuregawa, where the river-crossing services were closed due to high water. The water receded the following day, but the bridge collapsed; they therefore forded the river and spent the night in a town nearby. Entering Shimōsa province (east of Edo), they stopped over in Koga, crossed the Tone River by boat, passed the *sekisho* at Kurihashi and spent a night in Koshigaya. On the fifteenth, the women took a bath and fixed their hair at a Senju inn, then were escorted by the Matsumae officers into the Edo mansion of the domain. It had been a long journey of about thirty-five days.

Itsu and her companions stayed in Edo for a few weeks before leaving on 10.13 for Kyoto, their home. They traveled along the Tōkaidō, and climbed the dark hills of Hakone, lighting the road with pine tar torches. She wrote, "We, a party of three women alone, can thus travel the mountain road at night. How splendid is the reign of wise rulers!"

Itsu was fascinated by the scenery surrounding Miho-no-matsubara,[68] which made her forget all the fatigue and melancholy, and inspired her to compose more *waka* verses. They arrived in Kyoto eighteen days after leaving Edo.

Her diary, entitled "*Oku no araumi*" (Stormy Seas in the Far North), is an account of a long journey covering some 1600 kilometers. While the party experienced certain inconveniences caused by natural disaster, the three women were able to complete their journey safely without encountering any man-made hazards, an indication of the well-functioning administrative system under *bakuhan* rule.

Moving to a Husband's New Post

In 1806, Tsuchiya Ayako traveled to Sakai[69] in Izumi province following her husband Yasunao, who had been appointed the Sakai Magistrate.

The party left Edo on 4.4 and proceeded along the Tōkaidō. Clearing inspections at Hakone *sekisho*, they spent the night in an accommodation at the pass. While in Fuchū (present-day Shizuoka), they received gifts from the local magistrate and others. The city, in ancient times, was an outpost of the government that had created a centralized political system based on Chinese-style legal (*ritsuryō*) codes. In its more recent history, it was the place where Ieyasu, the founder of the Tokugawa *bakufu*, resided after his retirement. The richness of the land deeply impressed Ayako:

> This land is indeed beautiful, with its soil healthy in color and the trees and houses so charming. The young barley field spreads so vastly that it blends into the mist in the distance. Encouraged by yesterday's rain the farmers are energetically turning over the soil. A truly pleasant view it is. Sounds of busy weaving arise from various houses, and frogs croak loudly in the rice fields. People of this land are pleasant in appearance with lively voices. It is impossible to compare them to the poor peasants who were plowing the hilly land in Hakone.

Ayako could not help but contemplate the difference between the lifestyles of the people in Fuchū and those in the mountains of Hakone, whom she had just had occasion to observe. Then, they crossed the Abe River, which people were leisurely fording, thanks to the gentle winds that day. Ayako enjoyed the view from her palanquin, looking back from the opposite side of the river. The liveliness of this river crossing was another highlight of their visit to Fuchū, and she found it to be a far more exciting view than any other highway could offer. Almost everything about Fuchū interested her greatly.

At a seaside village, Ayako saw children selling seaweed, their clothes as shabby as their merchandise. Taking pity on them, she told her attendant to buy plenty of those for her; however the attendant's reply was dismissive, "For what? It's of no use," making Ayako feel indignant. Wherever they went she paid compassionate attention to the lives of impoverished people, writing in her diary, "I cannot help but sympathize with those people, wondering about the difficulties they have to overcome to earn their livelihood."

At Kanaya she gave a gratuity to her attendants and wrote letters to Edo, celebrating their successful crossing of the mountains of Hakone and the Ōi River, the two fiercest and strictest barriers along the Tōkaidō. The custom of tipping on such occasions was observed not only during official travel, but among common travelers as well, according to the book *Tōkaidō gojūsantsugi* (Fifty-three Stations along the Tōkaidō) by Kishii Yoshie.

When the party reached the steep slope of Sayo-no-Nakayama,[70] Ayako remembered the time when she had traveled the same area as a girl with her family. Twenty years later, she was now close to forty and tracing the same route. The memory left her nostalgic but also rather melancholy, as she pondered her life; as a woman she would follow her father in her youth and then her husband after marriage. The party crossed the Sea of Arai (Lake Hamana), where she underwent the *sekisho*'s routine inspection of women. In Akasaka there were prostitutes sending off their clients early in the morning, singing of the sorrow of parting, accompanied by the flute and *shamisen* (a three-string lute). Ayako observed the scene with mixed feelings, describing "an enchanting daybreak."

Along the way was Hōzō-ji, a temple of the Pure Land Sect, where the party stopped to appreciate the collection of articles left by Ieyasu. Ayako was moved to tears; her heart was filled with admiration and sympathy towards the founder of the Tokugawa *bakufu*, who was said to have devoted his life to ruling the country wisely. She left the temple reluctantly, urged by her entourage, looking back repeatedly.

Near Chirifu was Yatsuhashi, a historic spot where the ninth-century poet Ariwara no Narihira had composed a famous *waka* of traveler's gloom. Ayako desired to visit the place, but the plan was objected to by her male attendants, who, she observed, were obviously interested only in food and drink, with "no knowledge or taste whatsoever in poetic imagination or a graceful state of mind." Greatly annoyed, she wrote, "How difficult for a woman to have her way. I silently prayed to the Buddha to please let me be born a man in my next life."

Ayako offered an especially heartfelt prayer at Atsuta Shrine; it was where her ancestor Prime Minister Fujiwara Moronaga was banished by Taira no Kiyomori centuries before. Legend had it that Moronaga often visited the shrine, where he would view the moon while playing the *biwa* (a four-stringed Japanese lute) to console his aching heart.

From Miya,[71] a major post-station town on the Tōkaidō, Ayako's party departed in a large ferryboat provided by the Owari daimyo,[72] with the sailors singing to a lively drumbeat. The wind shifted along the way, forcing them to switch to a smaller boat, but they arrived at Kuwana safely. After overnighting at Kuwana and Kameyama, they passed the renowned Jizōin temple at Seki.[73] Then they finally climbed the steep mountain path leading to the Suzuka barrier, one of the most precipitously situated *sekisho* of the time. Ayako, who had until then favored ocean views, was amazed by the beauty of Mt. Fudesute, with the Suzuka River streaming into several branches, describing it "a superb sight of hills and rivers."

Their journey was not for recreation, however; therefore it did not allow Ayako time to tour Kyoto, nor to enjoy any of the famous sights near the capital before they sailed down the Yodo River. Disembarking at the Temma Bridge in Osaka, the party went straight to the official residence in Sakai, stopping only at Sumiyoshi Shrine along the way. By the town magistrate's office was a small gate leading to what was to be their residence. Entering the premises from the gate, Ayako found an old, forlorn building standing in a desolate garden with not a soul to be seen. She depicted the scene in a style reminiscent of classical Chinese prose:

> There is no one to be seen, nobody comes to meet us. The only answer is from the wind blowing through the pine tree, accompanied by the horrifying voice of a strange bird. Lamenting over the owl's crying in the pine and *katsura* trees, one stands alone in front of the stairs to see the house that is over two hundred years old with its gate broken on the ground. The shutters and sliding doors all decayed. No human footsteps are found on the moss-covered path, and thick ivy covers an aged pine tree. In the garden overgrown with weeds, the old owl in the tree is the voice that responds to their call.

Ayako was obviously standing overwhelmed in front of the decayed house that could in no way be compared to their mansion in Edo. She recorded her impressions in *waka*:

The rays of moonlight
leaking through the cracks
of the wooden walls,
I make them my friends to talk about
the melancholy of the days to come

People around her described Ayako as a "scholarly type, who keeps her husband under her thumb" or that "she does not get along well with her husband." But perhaps that very mental strength enabled her to overcome her situation and train in composing poems even in a moss-covered countrified house.

Her travel diary "*Tabi no inochige*" (A Journey with a Writing Brush) is a fine piece of work, vividly depicting in a flowery style the post stations and scenery along the Tōkaidō, and includes excellent scenic sketches and lyrical writing, allowing a glimpse into her rich imagination.

Following a Daimyo Transfer

In the eleventh month of 1845, the Akimoto clan of Yamagata domain in Dewa province[74] was ordered to transfer to Tatebayashi in Kōzuke province.[75] It had been eighty years since the last time such an order had been issued to the fiefdom; therefore, there was almost no one alive in the clan who had the experience of a daimyo transfer.

Naturally panic arose among the retainers and their families. Chaotic, though somewhat comical, situations arose. Quarrels began between debtors and creditors. Divorce was discussed between a retainer and his wife, who had originally been from a townsman's family. Some fled. Many lost their composure, fighting with their spouses. Old people lamented over the prospect of separation from their children's families. Merchants were already calculating how to profit from the chaos. Retainers would attempt to sell whatever they no longer needed to the merchants, but the samurai were no match for the crafty traders, suffering financial loss as a result. "They may be brave in heart but aren't glib talkers unfortunately," they would joke. Yamada Towako noted in her diary, "samurai's sad skill in trade—well, it is to sell valuables cheap and spend a fortune to purchase cheap stuff instead."

The family of Yamada Kidayū, who was in charge of the clan's finances and accounting, began their preparations for the move, as well. When spring arrived after the New Year's celebrations, their all-out efforts were accelerated. His wife Towako and the women of the household were extremely busy, running around during the day to obtain necessary items for the journey, and sewing travel attire for the family at night. Often Towako spent sleepless nights, thinking about countless things one after another, including what to do

about parting gifts for their friends and acquaintances. Invitations for farewell
parties began to arrive.

Now the first contingent of the clan began to leave. The Yamadas were invited to a farewell party thrown by the merchant house Ōsakaya, with whom
the family had developed a close relationship over the years. They partied at
Mt. Chitose, a scenic spot nearby, with mats spread out on the ground upon
which to sit. People enjoyed themselves to their hearts' content, feasting on
delicacies, drinking *sake*, and singing aloud. On another day the Yamadas
went to their family temple, offered prayers at the graves of their ancestors,
as well as their children who had died young, and bade them a final farewell.
As the day of departure approached, Towako would talk to even the trees and
grass in the backyard, saying good-bye to them, too.

On the first day of the fifth month, the Yamadas were to leave their house,
where they had lived for many years. Towako had to leave behind her beloved dog Chinko. She explained to the dog that she could not take her to
Tatebayashi, their new residence, because the people of the area preferred
foxes to dogs. She then gently advised her canine friend to be good and faithful to her new owners (a farmer's family nearby) and to behave herself so as
not to be scolded for stealing sandals. With tears streaming on her cheeks,
Towako thanked the dog for having been a faithful companion for such a long
time, and said good-bye to her. Then she stepped out of the house, but quickly
went back inside to offer a *kyōka* (a humorous verse in the form of *waka*)[76] to
the deity of poverty (*binbō-gami*)[77] of the house:

> Keep this old house
> where you've lived with us for so long
> as a gift from us,
> Pray stay for thousands of years to come
> do not bother to follow us to the new place

But this *binbō-gami* was quick in his reply message, teasing her.

> So coldheartedly
> you are going to leave me alone here,
> But let me tell you,
> your new honorable house there
> will be inhabited by my relatives as well

Towako, the fifty-two-year-old housewife of a samurai family, was obviously of a witty character; she could enjoy this one-woman act even in the
midst of chaotically busy days.

The banners of the incoming Mizuno clan were hung on the streets, and
curtains were stretched, dyed with the family crests of its high-ranking retain-

ers. The outgoing Akimoto clan took their temporary residence in the back streets, and Kawachiya Inn was assigned to accommodate the Yamadas. Curtains with the Yamada family crest were put up around the inn, somewhat reminiscent of a battlefield, to Towako's eyes. The town was enlivened with tall lanterns erected at street corners and people walking about beating clappers all night.

Kawachiya offered the Yamadas the guest rooms of their two-story storehouse and entertained the family warmly. Ōsakaya came to visit them for a formal farewell, bringing *sake* and delicacies. Other merchants also came to say good-bye, all bringing parting gifts.

On the fifth day of the fifth month the official delegation from Edo was to arrive in town for the transfer of the castle administration. Every household of the outgoing clan stopped its culinary activities in the morning, placed ceremonial mounds of sand at a corner of the house, and the master of the house alone waited in front of the gate, prostrate with broom in hand. An inspection of the castle was scheduled on the sixth, to be observed by officers from both clans. Towako's husband Kidayū was among them. He left for the castle, braving the weather in a raincoat, with ceremonial bow and gun in hand. Finally on the seventh, the delegation was to enter the castle. While the officers of both clans lined up beautifully in their magnificent formal attire and waited solemnly, the ceremony of castle transfer was completed successfully, creating a feeling of relief in the entire clan.

Towako's diary "*Dōchūki*" (A Record of Our Journey) meticulously depicts numerous informal events and affairs caused by the daimyo transfer, which would otherwise never have been known to us through official documents that record only formal political affairs. Her fresh and humorous style is very entertaining, conveying many very human aspects of the people of the time.

The Yamadas were assigned to leave as the eighth contingent on the eighteenth of the month. But unfortunately Towako caught a flu, which people suspected to have arrived with the Mizuno clan. The family decided that their son should leave first with his wife and child, and that Towako, her husband and their youngest son Tōichirō should leave later on the twenty-third, along with their family wardrobe chests.

On that day, the Yamadas expressed their profound gratitude to the people of Kawachiya, Ōsakaya, and the neighbors for their many kindnesses, and finally left Yamagata.

They took their lunch at Kameya Inn at the Kaminoyama hot spring resort. Safflowers were in full bloom along the road until Kamisekine. They stopped over at Narage for the first overnight of the journey. The inn owner generously offered *sake* with dinner as a farewell treat. At another inn at Kanayama, the owner received the family with great courtesy, clad in full formal attire. He served *sake*, side dishes, and various delicacies, among which were boiled green peas, rice cakes with plenty of white sugar topping, and arrowroot-starch cakes, the local specialty, all displayed on an elegant one-legged table for each person.

They crossed the Kanayama Pass and refreshed themselves at a tea stall in the area of Namezu. The owner unfortunately had nothing special to offer and all he could serve was two pickled plums. Trying to sooth their empty stomachs, they opened their baggage and munched on pickles and ginger-flavored *miso*, which Kawachiya and Ōsakaya had prepared for them.

They spent the night of the twenty-fourth at an inn in Watase. On that day Towako was bitten by a horsefly, which had flown into her palanquin while she was dozing off. The bite swelled up and Towako suffered from the pain for about three days. Approaching the Shin Pass the following day, they were awed by a magnificent landscape of boulders called *zaimoku-iwa* (lumber boulders), which soared straight against the sky just like boards lined up vertically. When passing villages in Shimotozawa and Kamitozawa, they were annoyed by the smoke and sulfur-like smell coming from the silver refinery. They lunched at an inn on the Kosaka Pass. A vendor was walking about selling *kōri* (ice) in the town of Kōri, which Towako found amusing, buying some to temper the heat. They spent the night at Shishidoya Inn in Senoue. The establishment had many rooms; it also housed about ten harlots. Towako was carrying a rabbit with her when she arrived at the inn. She had found the animal the previous day when traveling over the mountains, and had it caught for her to make it a souvenir for her grandchildren. She borrowed a basket from the inn master to keep the rabbit overnight, but was greatly disappointed later to discover it had escaped.

On the twenty-sixth, the family passed the castle of Fukushima and spent the night in another castle town, Nihonmatsu. When passing through the town, she saw dogs being hunted and captured by town officials. Towako's heart broke when she learned that their lord hated dogs and ordered the hunt. She also noticed about ten homeless beggars grilling some food in the precinct of the Sugita-Yakushi temple. Their lunch break that day was at Kōriyama, where once again they saw vendors selling *kōri*.

On their way through a town called Sasagawa, a thunderstorm hit, rattling Towako, who hated thunder more than anything. The party took shelter from the storm in a nearby tea stall, had the owner close the wooden shutters and burn incense for them, where Towako frantically chanted sutras until she almost lost her voice. She held on to the incense and repeatedly lighted it on the way to the next destination, Sukagawa. Sukagawa was the halfway point of their journey; the Yamadas tipped their retainers and maids to celebrate their safe journey so far.

They spent the next night at the designated daimyo inn (*honjin*) in Shira-saka. The inn was beautifully furnished and had a magnificent garden. The house had two so-called "serving girls" (prostitutes).[78] They served meals for the family, but Towako found the women ill-mannered. At Maruya Inn in Ashino, too, where they took their lunch, she saw two serving girls; this time, though, Towako ended up enjoying chatting with one of them, who turned out to also be from Yamagata. The girl even knew the wife of Ōsakaya. On that day the Yamada party passed a contingent of the Mizuno clan, who were heading in the opposite direction on their way to Yamagata. Some in the pro-cession appeared exhausted traveling on foot while others were being carried in palanquins with the family crest posted on them. The Yamadas stayed in the *honjin* at another town that night, where they saw yet another set of two serving girls.

On 6.1, they were to cross the Nakagawa River but found only two ferry boats available; it therefore took hours for the wardrobes and palanquins to be carried across the river. Then they headed for Kitsuregawa to lodge at the *honjin* there.

At the *honjin*, there was a girl of about ten years old who came to serve them, and Towako gave some sweets to the child. The next day they visited a shrine in Utsunomiya to offer prayers. The town was very lively, with nu-merous shops lining the streets. It looked just like a beautiful *ukiyoe* painting, exclaimed Towako. When they spent a night in Suzumenomiya, Towako again encountered two serving girls at their inn. After passing Koyama the next day, they lodged in Furukawa.

On the fourth day of the month, they passed the castle of Tatebayashi, viewing the beautiful white lotus blossoms in the moat. Now they finally entered the castle town, where they were welcomed by earlier-arriving family members, and together they rejoiced over the safe trip.

In Towako's diary "*Dōchūki*," which includes *waka* and *kyōka*, there are also close to seventy black-and-white ink paintings. Her paintings cover a variety of themes: people relaxing in hot springs, the furniture and gardens of the inns, and scenes from river ferries and castle towns. Her artwork captures not only the magnificence of nature, but also people's postures, their coif-fures, and the patterns of the kimono and sashes that they wore. Altogether, her entire travel diary is a brilliant piece of work that could also be a rich source for folkloric studies.

A Bride's Journey

Fujiki Ichi, the daughter of a chief retainer of Aizu domain, was separated from her father in childhood and grew up with her mother's natal family, the

Fujikis, in Kyoto. Her father, Hoshina Masaoki, had fallen from power and
been banished to Mizusawa in Ogawashō (in present-day Niigata prefecture),
across the Agano River. Her maternal grandfather was the chief priest of
Kamigamo Shrine.

When she was fourteen, Ichi's marriage was arranged to the eldest son
of the Kishi clan, a chief retainer of Kurume domain in Chikugo province
(Kyūshū). Ichi recorded an account of her journey as a bride:

> It wasn't that I attempted to follow the example of famous writings of olden
> times, but I simply wanted to keep a journal to console my melancholy mind
> during the journey.

Thus begins the diary of a girl who left the house of her mother and grandfather to travel to a strange and faraway land. It vividly depicts her longing
for the capital, where she had grown up, and anxiety for the future.

At the end of the year 1700, the bride's procession made a torchlit journey
to Fushimi, and then headed for Naniwa (old name of Osaka) by boat. At the
mouth of the river, Ichi parted with her maids, who had come that far to see
her off. The boat sailed further and further from the capital, passing famous
scenic spots in the Seto Inland Sea, such as Naruo, Nishinomiya, Wada-no-
misaki, Suma, and Akashi. Ichi's homesickness intensified.

> Sea breeze of Onoura—
> you blow far, away from me
> as our procession moves forward,
> Pray, tell my people there
> of my longing for home

Various landscapes impressed her, however. She found Akashi Bay too
splendid for words, and Awaji Island was "one thousand times" more beautiful than she had imagined while living in Kyoto.

On 12.29, the ship anchored at Murozumi, deviating from the original itinerary, which had them stopping at Kaminoseki.[79] Ichi took a great liking to
the place, describing it as "a charming beach, indeed." The sea was dotted by
Kasadoshima and other small islands, and on land, luxuriant with evergreen
trees, the *fugen-bosatsu* (Samantabhadra) was enshrined at a local temple.
The party could not depart on New Year's Eve due to lack of wind and
therefore ended up welcoming the New Year there. The boatmen ceremoniously dedicated young *sake* to the spirit of the ship, erected auspicious pine
branches at bow and stern, and enshrined a guardian deity in the boat. Ichi
observed, fascinated.

With no wind, the surface of the water in Murozumi Bay was like a polished mirror, and the mist hanging over the pine trees on the shore pleased Ichi's eyes. But they could not resume the voyage for ten long days due to a continued dead calm.

On the tenth day of the first month they finally arrived at Kokura in Buzen province, where Ichi was met by a messenger from the Arima clan of Kurume domain; the Arimas were to assume the role of Ichi's guardians at the wedding. Led by the messenger, Ichi's overland journey began. The party overnighted at Koyase and Yamae[80] along the way. In those places Ichi was intrigued by an unusual sight.

> When passing the area called Ishizaka, I noticed smoke coming up with a terrible odor from the tiny, run-down houses. I asked the messenger about it, who explained to me that the residents there burned stone instead of wood for cooking, which was the source of the smell. I felt sorry for the people who had to live in such an environment, but perhaps they were so accustomed to it that they might not be bothered so much.

Ichi expressed youthful compassion for the commoners in the Chikuhō district, where coal was already in daily use at the time.[81]

After stopping over at Matsuzaki, she arrived at her guardians' residence, where she formally entered. On the same day, she headed for the residence of the Kishis, the bridegroom's family.

Few accounts of brides' journeys have so far been discovered. Ichi's diary of her twenty-five-day travel, therefore, is an important record, especially in light of her tender age. To date, four handwritten copies of this diary have been found, and their varying postscripts indicate how her diary has been preserved until today. By reading the postscripts, we also learn that there were dramatic developments later on in the author's life. One small work of literature indeed offers us a glimpse of a substantial slice of history.

Travel under Escort

Kurosawa Toki, mentioned earlier, was finally able to secure the safe delivery of her poem of appeal; it would be handed by a friend of hers to a high-ranking court aristocrat, who would then submit it to the Emperor. Relaxing afterward at a friend's house in Osaka, she could afford a little time for recreation, and she met with like-minded people to compose *haikai*. On 1859.4.1, as she was walking back from a bathhouse with her friend's old mother, Toki was stopped by two officers. They called out, "We are here to escort you for questioning upon the request of the Kyoto office," and arrested her on the spot. She was taken for investigation to both the Osaka and Kyoto Magistrates. Officers repeatedly interrogated Toki with the same questions; they suspected that she was a secret agent of Nariaki's wife Yoshiko, who was the daughter of the aristocratic Arisugawa family, relations of the Emperor, or that there was a secret message encoded in her poem. They also demanded that she confess her accomplice's name. Toki did not cave in under the harsh questioning, claiming that she acted of her own will and for the sake of the country. The investigation continued over forty days. Then she was informed that the case would be jointly further examined by three authorities: the Edo Magistrate, the Magistrate of Temples and Shrines, and the Magistrate of Finance. There was at the time a method of transferring criminals using bamboo cages (called *tōmaru-kago*), and Toki was sent to Edo in a *tōmaru* cage under tight security.

> At the post stations along the Tōkaidō, I saw town officers equipped with batons. Their attendants were guarding them and calling out to the unruly half-naked vagabonds on the street to prostrate, as if we were a daimyo procession. The cage bearers rushed along the highway like flying birds, without stopping at rest areas, only switching the carrying bar from shoulder to shoulder. An attendant was sent on horseback to the inn to announce our approach. We arrived at four o'clock.

The cage was carried into the inn with Toki inside, six men assigned to guard her cage through the night.

When passing through castle towns, they were greeted by the chief retainer followed by a number of attendants. People on the street withdrew, nobody daring to cross, while numerous onlookers came out and prostrated themselves under the eaves of the houses. This carefully guarded journey was hard on Toki, who had a chronic health condition, but an old man called Senzō, assigned as her caretaker, and other officers looked after her kindly. After thirteen days in the bamboo cage, Toki's journey along the Tōkaidō ended.

She was detained in a jail for the sick in Asakusa (northeastern Edo) with three female guards. In the sixth month, Toki was summoned to the court, where the three Magistrates and a number of daimyo were all in attendance. Matsudaira Hōki-no-kami, Magistrate of Temples and Shrines, represented them and questioned her directly. She appealed to him that her actions had been motivated by the belief that "I may be a humble individual, but am a loyal subject of the Emperor" for whom "This is a time of crisis." The Magistrate closed his eyes for a while before he announced, fighting back tears, "There is no sensible human being who does not revere the Imperial Court." He then opened the sliding door behind him and retreated into the back room abruptly, leaving the daimyo in attendance sitting silently, not knowing what to do.

While in jail, Toki's conditions worsened, and she was seriously ill for more than two months. Her detention was extended. When she miraculously recovered, Toki was transferred to another detention house in Denmachō, central Edo. In the middle of the tenth month, she was summoned, along with ten other political prisoners, including Yoshida Shōin[82] for further investigation. At night, by lantern light, she was questioned about her poem of appeal to the Emperor, and then returned to the jail in Denmachō.

On 10.27, after seven months' imprisonment, Toki was sentenced to mid-level banishment (*chū-tsuihō*); it banned her from entering the forty-square-kilometer area of Edo with Nihonbashi as its center. She was also denied entry to Yamashiro province including Kyoto and her home province Hitachi. On the same day, she heard an officer read in a ringing voice the death sentence for Yoshida Shōin. Toki left the jail with a person who had come to escort her, and they headed for Suzukōya, her hometown. After three days' journey she stopped over at Motegimura in Shimotsuke, where she stayed for three days. She secretly entered her hometown on 11.6.

Toki recorded her account of the experience of those seven months away from home as a captive, entitling the diary "*Toraware no fumi*" (A Captive's Diary).

Refugees from the Boshin War

The transfer of power from Tokugawa to the new Meiji government was tumultuous. In 1867.10, in a formal letter to the Imperial Court, the fifteenth shogun Tokugawa Yoshinobu conveyed his decision to return sovereign power to the Emperor. On 12.9, the Imperial Court proclaimed the restoration of imperial power. In less than a month however, on 1868.1.3, a *bakufu* army clashed with the united forces of Satsuma and Chōshū domains in Kyoto; it was the beginning of the Toba-Fushimi battle, the initial armed clash in the Boshin War, which would eventually last eighteen months until 1869.5 when the battle in Hakodate ended.[83] Numerous people lost their lives during the war. Satsuma and Chōshū were the major players in the new government with the backing of the Imperial Court; they therefore aimed at overthrowing, rather than coexisting with, the Tokugawa shogunate. They announced punishment for those considered enemies of the Emperor; among those named were the shogun Yoshinobu, the domains of Aizu and Kuwana, which had fired against the Imperial army in the Toba-Fushimi battle, and other domains that had allegedly demonstrated hostility towards the new government. Most daimyo west of the Kansai region quickly swore allegiance to the Imperial government and joined, one after another, expeditions to bring Edo and the eastern domains under control.

Edo Castle surrendered on 1868.4.11. Aizu domain petitioned the new government repeatedly for acceptance of its surrender and apology, but all its petitions were rejected. Then, daimyo of the northeastern region formed the League of Ōu Major Domains (*Ōu reppan dōmei*) to confront the new Imperial government.

But one after another the castles of Nagaoka, Niigata and Nihonmatsu fell, and on 9.22, Aizu finally surrendered to the relentless attacks after a one-month siege.

Women and children, too, were dragged into the war, sometimes not even fully comprehending the causes for which their men were fighting. Fleeing the battles' fires, searching desperately for shelter, a number of women wrote memoirs of the horrifying days they experienced far from home.

Numata Kōsetsu relates her experience as a refugee in *"Kōchōen tsur-ezuregusa"* (Essays in Idleness in the Desolate Garden). She fled the town of Yokote, whose castle had been attacked by the League of Ōu Major Domains because their daimyo had sided with the new government. Her husband was killed in the battle. Kōsetsu wandered the nearby villages searching for an appropriate location to bury her husband's head, which she had wrapped in cloth and carried along with her. Suzuki Mitsuko, the daughter of an Aizu retainer, who was only eight years old at the time of the war, composed a memoir later. Hyūga Yuki, who was also young, wrote an account of her experience later in a memoir entitled *"Omoto"* (An Evergreen). Hyūga Rin's memories were recorded by the wives of Aizu retainers. Among additional accounts of the war are *"Matsu no ochiba"* (Fallen Pine Needles) by Teshirogi Kiyoko, *"Kaikyūdan"* (My Memoir) by Takeda Take, *"Konjaku omoidashi-ki"* (My Memories, Old and New), an autobiography of Takahashi Ryūden, *"Yōji o tsurete Aizu-sensō o nogareshi tōji"* (Fleeing the Aizu War with An Infant) by Hasegawa Mitoko, and many more.

Fleeing Battlefields with Children

Gunfire flared in the castle town of Nagaoka in Echigo province at the beginning of the fifth month. Koganei Yukiko, the wife of a retainer, left home with three sons, aged twelve, nine, and five, and a two-year-old daughter in tow. She headed for a village where a family acquaintance resided. Inspections by the Imperial army were fiercely strict, making their stay at the acquaintance's home difficult. They fled to a hut deep in the mountains, with the boys' heads shaved to disguise them as country boys. There, Yukiko prepared meals for herself and the children, rinsing rice with the water from the brook nearby and picking grass from the field to accompany it. Soon, she began to see the enemy's bonfire every night on the ridge of the mountain ahead. Their hideout was no longer safe. They left the hut to rely on another acquaintance, who also turned out to be unable to offer safe haven. She made up her mind that the only option was to escape to Aizu, leaving the two-year-old daughter under the foster care of a farmer's family who had assisted them early on. Yukiko hired a village man to send the daughter to the farmer's house.

> Heartbreaking
> is the smile of my infant daughter,
> sucking milk from breast
> not knowing she is soon
> to part with her mother

Her daughter, oblivious to the situation, left smiling, carried on the back of the man. The mother and three sons clambered over the hills, stumbling and falling. The route had been named *hachijūri-goe* (80 *ri* crossing) because of its steep undulations, where one *ri* (4 km) would equal ten *ri* of normal road. At the top of the pass was a *sekisho*, where a guard recorded Yukiko as "a woman carrying both long and short swords (as a samurai does)." The *sekisho* had a rescue hut installed for refugees on its premises. Yukiko washed her sons' clothes in a pond nearby and dried them in the heat of a wood fire. The mother and sons spent several days in the villages of Aizu domain and then headed for the castle town. But on that very day, Aizu was occupied by enemy forces. They changed their plan and headed for Yonezawa. While climbing the steep Hibara Pass, the bottoms of their straw sandals broke, leaving their feet exposed and bleeding. On their way they learned that Yonezawa was not a safe place for them, either. They changed destination again, this time for Sendai.

They struggled along and finally arrived in Sendai, but the city was in chaos with refugees pouring in from various provinces. By coincidence, Yukiko was reunited with her husband, who had escorted his lord there. After a brief meeting, however, they had to separate once again. Yukiko continued the journey with her sons to Matsushima.

The surface of the quiet sea shined like a mirror, reflecting the fresh green of the pine grove. Far offshore stood Kinkasan, the island lush green like a beautiful painting. I felt complete empathy with Bashō, who could not compose even one verse when he passed this area, overwhelmed with its superb beauty. [84]

> How could I have
> imagined I'd see Matsushima
> on such a dreadful journey,
> the magnificent sight I had
> dreamed of for many a year

When living comfortably in their Nagaoka residence, thought Yukiko, she had seldom had the opportunity to go out nor had the boys even seen the sea at Niigata, but now on this tough journey seeking refuge, she was, ironically, able to appreciate the beauty of Matsushima. In spite of the harsh circumstances, lacking even food, clothing, and shelter, Yukiko preserved her reflective calm, and was able to sustain the refined worldview that brought to her mind the anecdote of Bashō, the revered *haikai* poet.

The mother and her sons trudged on, occasionally seeking shelter at fishermen's houses. At one point they were instructed to go to Ōhara in Esashi,[85] one hundred kilometers away. After several days of walking they reached the mountain village, where some three hundred refugees were living in an old temple, and where thirty people slept upon a mere eight *tatami* mats.[86]

That year the enemies came to reconciliation at last. Yukiko went home to Nagaoka with her family at the end of the year.

Under extreme circumstances, material and mental, Yukiko and her children, with their fellow refugees, learned to live rough, with none of the usual privileges of the samurai class, dependent on the many kindnesses offered by people of different classes and regions.

"Come my grandchildren, gather around this fireplace," begins Yukiko's story of the Boshin War. It was her daughter-in-law Kimiko who recorded her narrative as "*Boshin no mukashigatari*" (Olden Days of the Boshin War). Kimiko was the younger sister of Mori Ōgai and a Meiji literary figure herself.[87] She wrote of Yukiko's heart-wrenching experiences in a beautifully fluent style, connecting powerfully with her readers.

Leading a Family in Exile

On the twenty-third day of the eighth month of 1868, fire bells sounded and the castle town of Aizu fell under attack, people fleeing chaotically in the rain. Mitsu, thirty-nine years old, the older sister of a retainer, packed up her family's belongings in the midst of gunfire and entered the castle, where women nursed the injured, prepared food, and made bullets under the instruction of the chief lady-in-waiting and other supervisors. People's hearts lightened when Mitsu's younger sister Kiyo, who had married into the Akabane family, gave birth to a girl in the castle. Outside the castle on that same day occurred a tragic incident; many of the retainers' women and children set fire to their own houses and killed themselves as Imperial forces were about to invade the town.

After a one-month siege the castle surrendered on 9.22. Daimyo Matsudaira Katamori and his sister-in-law Teruhime were moved to the Myōkoku-ji temple for confinement. Aizu retainers were transferred to Inawashiro, Shiokawa, and other areas to be placed under the supervision of the new Imperial government. Women were allocated to nearby villages.

Mitsu's family of six (five women and one-year-old Seikichi), along with relatives, was sent to the village headman's house in Oyamamura. There, her younger sister Yū died. Later they were instructed to move to another village, where they borrowed a room at the house of villager Ishiyama Tadaemon. Her folks fell ill one after another, and the infant suffered malnutrition, unable to receive enough breast milk from his ailing mother. To feed the boy, they mixed glutinous malt-sugar into a sweet drink made from fermented rice. In the meantime, peasant riots erupted in various villages. Rioters would swarm village headmen's houses, drag out various items from the warehouses, burn them in the backyards, shave the wooden pillars, and set fire to the doors and paper screens. Mitsu and her folks were terrified when a riot broke out in a neighboring village. Reportedly rioters would not harm women and children; nevertheless they were ordered not to leave the house.

Their lord Matsudaira Katamori was still in confinement when his heir Kataharu was born in the sixth month of 1869, the second year of Meiji. In the eleventh month, the continuation of the family name and the succession to the headship of the clan was granted to Kataharu. The child-heir was given Tonami of the Shimokita Peninsula (the northernmost region of Honshū) as his new fief, which yielded thirty thousand *koku*[88] of rice. Clansmen began to emigrate in the fourth month of the following year.

Mitsu and her family left on 10.11, traveling overland north to Tonami. On the way they spent nights at Inawashiro, Nihonmatsu, Fukushima and Morioka. The hilly route between Numakunai and Ichinohe was a tough road, wrote Mitsu, where they were rained upon and developed blisters on their feet. As a party of mostly women and the aged, they had difficulties obtaining palanquins whichever road they took.

Once in Tonami they were allocated lodging in a villager's house in Sannohe. On a market day, Mitsu saw cakes made of bracken-root starch sprinkled with sugar and soybean flour, which was used as a substitute food at the time of a bad harvest. Curious, she bought a few. Their life in the village was incredibly inconvenient. For example, they did not have easy access to water and had to carry it more than a hundred meters from a spring. Mitsu petitioned to the village office; then they were transferred to a family in another village. During the winter they earned money by spinning, but had a harder time in summer when no jobs were available. Everything was different. People spoke with strange accents, dressed and applied makeup differently, which "struck me as so weird until I became used to them," as she wrote. Food was another challenge. Things they wanted to eat, such as *daikon* radish, were hard to obtain since the local people would buy them all before they could. Mitsu's family often ended up eating cheap soybeans and *azuki* red beans, earning an unfriendly nickname from the locals "the bean eaters from Aizu." She lamented in her diary, "We were totally perplexed by various inconveniences here in Nanbu domain." But she was also interested in their customs: "They call the fifteenth of the first month Women's New Year's Day, celebrating merrily until the twenty-first, just like the first week of the month, and play on the twenty-second, just like they do on the eighth. They feed ravens with rice cakes from their hands, and men also come out from each house. It is indeed a lively scene."

In 1873, the sixth year of Meiji, the rations from the new government, four cups of brown rice and two hundred *mon* (the local currency) per person, stopped with a notice that those who wished to return to Aizu should report to the authorities. Mitsu's family discussed the matter and decided to go back, particularly for the education of Seikichi, the family heir. Until the date of departure, the women of the family made their living by peddling eggs, which they purchased at a faraway village.

The family left the village along with another party on 4.19 of the following year. Seven-year-old Seikichi and his mother traveled on horseback, the other women on foot. They first stopped over at Numakunai, then Morioka, where they met other parties also returning to Aizu. They all continued the journey together, sailing down the Kitakami River and lodging at Mizusawa and Ichinoseki. They got off the boat at Ishinomaki. Walking about the port city, Mitsu was amazed at its prosperity and the abundance of novel merchandise. It was completely different from the remote villages in Sannohe, wrote Mitsu, "People's manners are refined, unlike those in Nanbu. The smell of musk, people's hair styles, etc., all impressed me a great deal." They spent a night at Onojuku, took a small boat to Shiogama, and enjoyed the view of Matsushima, listening to the skipper's entertaining explanations. After sightseeing in Shiogama, Mitsu had sea bream cooked by a fisherman and hosted the party to feast upon the delicacy. Heading for Sendai, the group was amazed at the new-fangled rickshaws[89] operating along the road lined with pine trees. Sendai, the major city in Ōshū, was already in tune with the new era, while in the countryside of Nanbu, people's life-style still remained unchanged even under the new government.

Stopping over at several towns on their way, the party rested at the hot springs of Bandai-Atami. On the following day, everyone, including the aged, crossed over the Nakayama Pass on foot, since the road was too challenging to cross on horseback. They stayed overnight at Sekiwaki by Lake Inawashiro, then paid a visit to Mt. Mine, but its shrine[90] had been burned in the war, leaving only ruins. After a night at a local village, the party arrived at their acquaintance's house in Aizu, whom they had asked for accommodation in advance. Unfortunately, however, they found that not only was the wife of the house seriously ill but the place was overcrowded with their relatives repatriated from Tonami. Mitsu and her family searched for another shelter and finally settled at the place of Ishiyama Tadaemon of Idemura, who had looked after them before they had left for Tonami.

It had been five years and nine months since Mitsu's family was driven from their longtime residence in Aizu by the invasion of the Imperial army. During those years, the family lost many of its members. Mitsu's younger brother Iwagorō, who had inherited the family estate, was killed in the fierce battle at Chōmei-ji on 8.29. Her other younger brother was among the soldiers of *Byakkotai* (an army formed by teenage boys of Aizu), who killed themselves en mass at Mt. Iimori before the surrender. Her father Shinbei was killed by artillery fire on 9.14 in the castle during the siege. Yū, her younger sister, died of illness during their exile when no sufficient food or medicine was available. It was only a baby and women who survived: Iwagorō's son Seikichi, who was four months old when they left Aizu, her mother who was almost sixty years old, three younger sisters, and Mitsu herself. Mitsu, as the oldest daughter of the Mases, led the family through those difficult years. She scraped out a living while her family frequently moved from one place to another as refugees; she constantly encouraged Iwagorō's young widow, her sister-in-law, helping to nurture the infant Seikichi; and finally managed their homecoming to Aizu after a long absence. Her travel diary "*Boshin-go zakki*" (Miscellaneous Notes after the Boshin War) records her experiences of those nearly seven years and illuminates Mitsu's role as the rock of the family during those years. It is also testimony to the marks of resilient women who helped themselves as well as others throughout the war and its aftermath.

A Messenger to Save the Tokugawa

Edo was in an uproar in the spring of 1868. A rumor reached the shogun's inner palace that the Imperial army's all-out attack was imminent, and the women of Edo Castle desperately counted on Princess Kazunomiya to resolve the situation.

It had been six years since Kazunomiya, the younger sister of Emperor Kōmei, had wed then-shogun Tokugawa Iemochi. It was a political marriage intended to unite the Imperial Court and the shogunate, but both Iemochi and the Emperor had since passed away. The widowed princess, now tonsured and called Seikan-in, had led a quiet life in the inner palace of Edo Castle, where her mother-in-law Tenshō-in and consorts of late shoguns had also resided. But now many people began to call on her, requesting her mediation with the Imperial Court. Among them were frequent messengers from Shogun Yoshinobu with his letter of apology and from Tenshō-in with her petition for the continuation of the Tokugawa clan. The princess, who had refrained from taking any public role, finally decided to attempt assistance. She chose Tsuchimikado Fujiko as her emissary to deliver her letters to Kyoto. Fujiko was a high-ranking lady-in-waiting who had earned Kazunomiya's full confidence after the deaths of the princess's mother and her chief lady-in-waiting.

Fujiko placed three letters in a bamboo letter box. Two were from the princess addressed to her uncle Hashimoto Saneakira, the Major Councilor, and her nephew Saneyana, the Minor Captain, respectively; the other was a petition from Yoshinobu, the shogun. She left the castle on 1868.1.26. On the twenty-ninth, when she reached Atsutajuku in the rain, Fujiko learned that governor-general Saneyana had come as far as Kuwana to pacify the Tōkaidō. She dispatched a messenger to him requesting an audience; she then traveled overland along the Sayakaidō on 2.1 and waited for Saneyana's reply at Sayajuku. A message came from Saneyana that he would wait for her at Kōtoku-ji in Kuwana. She met him at the temple, but Saneyana's anger toward Yoshinobu was so profound that Fujiko hesitated to even submit the shogun's letter of petition. She handed him the confidential letter from the princess addressed to him:

> It is indeed understandable that Yoshinobu himself deserves punishment, as, aside from the latest incident, he has repeatedly demonstrated disrespectful behavior toward the Imperial Court. However, I sincerely petition to you to please grant the continuation of the Tokugawa clan. It will truly be a regretful situation if the Tokugawa are disgraced as enemies of the Imperial house for generations to come. Here, I would risk my life to implore you to please, out of pity for me, allow the Tokugawa to vindicate their honor and see the family name continue. Should the Imperial army be sent to attack Edo Castle, I would certainly cast in my lot with the Tokugawa, for it would be truly regretful to see myself alone survive while witnessing the collapse of the entire clan. While I would not hold my own life dear, I am deeply unwilling to disrespect the Imperial Court by sharing my fate with that of its enemy.

The letter above, quoted from *Seikan-in no miya on-nikki* (Diary of Princess Seikan-in), demonstrates the princess's determination to throw in her lot with the Tokugawa clan, into which she was married. It appears that the Imperial princess acquired the attitude typical of samurai-class women; highly virtuous and selfless, and bearing a strong feeling of responsibility toward continuation of the family name.

Completing her meeting with Saneyana, Fujiko stayed that night at the Kenpon-ji temple in Kuwana. She continued her journey along the Tōkaidō, stopping over at Yokkaichi, Tsuchiyama, Ishibe, Ōtsu, and arrived at Kyoto on the sixth. Immediately, she started to sound the Imperial Court on the princess's letters, meeting with relevant people such as the Hases, who were in an important position in the new government, the Kurahashis and the Nakanoins, high-ranking court nobles, and former ladies-in-waiting. Fujiko worked until late, seldom coming home before midnight; it was often past four o'clock in the morning when she could finally go to bed after recording an account of the day at the house of her natal Tsuchimikado family. On the sixteenth, she met with Saneakira once more through the good offices of her older brother Tsuchimikado Haruo, when Saneakira handed her a memo from Ōgimachi Sanjō Sanenaru. It was an unofficial notice to grant the continuation of the Tokugawa clan. Fujiko left immediately, bearing the memo, for Edo.

She left rainy Kyoto on the eighteenth. On the twenty-third, Fujiko met with Saneyana again at Araijuku, where she returned the travel permission seal she had borrowed on her way to Kyoto, and was now given another seal for her return trip to Edo. She had intended to lodge in Fuchūjuku on the twenty-fifth but altered her plan to stay in Koyoshida, one station closer to Kyoto, since Fuchūjuku was crowded with the Satsuma-Chōshū contingent, the spearhead of the Imperial army for the eastern expedition. On the twenty-ninth she arrived in Edo and immediately reported to the princess, submitting to her the memo from Sanjō Sanenaru.

In the third month, the spearheads of the punitive force were approaching Edo, with the Tōzandō squad reaching Itabashi, the Tōkaidō squad nearing the Rokugō River, and the Hokurikudō squad as close as Senju. The princess feared that if an all-out attack on the shogunate capital were to take place *bakufu* retainers and the citizens of Edo might resist and riot. That would certainly be behavior disrespectful to the Imperial Court and a reason for the court to revoke its permission for the continuance of the Tokugawa, a profoundly serious consequence that had to be avoided by all means. She wrote another confidential letter to Saneyana, imploring him to "please delay the advance of the army," for she would devote all her efforts to ensuring the obedience of the Tokugawa clan and the appeasement of the citizens of Edo. Once again she dispatched Fujiko to the Minor Captain as her messenger.

On 3.10, Fujiko left Edo Castle, passed Shinagawa and reached the Rokugō ferry (at the lower reaches of the Tama River), where she observed that the far bank of the river was strictly guarded by Satsuma troops. Beyond the troops, a checkpoint was set up and a camp pitched in Kawasaki. Her attendants announced that they were the "party of Mme. Fujiko, emissary of Princess Seikan-in," but the guard would not allow them to pass, demanding,

"Your honor, we cannot issue permission for your passage without hearing the purpose of your travel." There happened to be an officer named Yamaguchi to whom they explained their mission in detail. Finally, they were allowed to pass. On that day they canceled their planned stay at Totsuka, and arrived in Kanagawa in the evening. Anticipating further difficulties ahead, Fujiko wrote a letter to the Minor Captain requesting that he facilitate their journey. They were stopped again the next day at a checkpoint. Indeed, checkpoints were everywhere, slowing their travel substantially. In Fujisawa, where the party was stopped and could not move ahead, two warning shots were fired from a cannon in the camp, terrifying her women attendants. They took the road that ran closer to Ōiso, tipped by the local people that there would be no checkpoints along that route. It was a bumpy and messy road, and they arrived at Iwamoto-in at Enoshima Island[91] in the twilight.

According to their guide, however, the army was apparently going to build barricades the next day between Ōiso and Nangō, and station soldiers there. The party therefore left the island in haste at about two that morning. In heavy rain and without rain gear, they hurriedly made their way, arriving in Ōiso at dawn, and then continued as far as Odawara. The party was invited to lodge at the *honjin*, courtesy of Odawara clansmen who were guarding the area; now they could rest and dry their clothes. Fujiko wrote a letter to the princess. On the thirteenth, they left Odawara in the morning, passed Hakone and reached Numazu via Mishima without incident. Numazu was where the Minor Captain established his camp as commander of the Tōkaidō squad, closely guarded, and surrounded by a stretched curtain. Fujiko's party stayed at Sōhaku-ji that night.

The following day, the fourteenth, Hashimoto Saneyana came to the temple to meet with them, guarded by his attendants. He told Fujiko that the army would not resort to the use of force without provocation and therefore, he said, it was critical for the *bakufu* to pacify Edo. He also advised that she should leave Numazu right away, since it was her enemy's headquarters, and return to Edo. Completing her mission, Fujiko left Numazu on the fifteenth, stayed at Odawara and Hodogaya, and arrived at Edo Castle on the seventeenth. She reported to the princess and submitted to her the response from Saneyana.

On the same day Fujiko met with Saneyana, a meeting between Saigō Takamori[92] and Katsu Kaishū[93] was held at the Satsuma domain Edo residence; the two men, representing the new government and the shogunate respectively, came to an agreement regarding the conditions for the latter's surrender. Thus the full-scale offensive on Edo scheduled for the fifteenth was called off at the last moment.

The historic meeting of Saigō and Katsu has been spotlighted and widely praised; there is a famous painting of the scene as well, giving the impression that the two men alone had achieved the bloodless surrender of Edo Castle. We learn, however, that there were also women who made desperate efforts toward that objective, as clearly described in Fujiko's travel diary "*Tsuchimikado Fujiko hikki*" (The Note of Tsuchimikado Fujiko).

TRAVEL OF DAIMYO FAMILIES

Overview

Of the travel diaries I have so far collected, approximately one third were written by women of the samurai class; furthermore, one third of that group were of daimyo families. The actual population of daimyo families was tiny, probably one several-hundredth of the samurai class.

Considering that the samurai class was a little under ten percent of Japan's entire population of the time, the number of travel diaries by women of daimyo families is rather significant in my current collection: eighteen written by sixteen authors, out of well over one hundred works. Of course, there was another genre in which they created a much larger collection of works, specifically *waka*. *Waka* was a part of the very basic education for both men and women of the daimyo class; having been trained since childhood, it would have been highly unlikely that any one of them would be incapable of producing at least a few verses should the occasion arise. Women's *waka* are found in abundance, indeed, if one digs into the archives of any daimyo family.

Now setting *waka* collections aside, the existence of their travel diaries indicates that not only were these women cultured enough to write prose in addition to composing *waka*, but were allowed a certain degree of freedom to roam, or in some cases they found themselves in unfortunate political circumstances that forced them to travel.

Their accounts of travel can be roughly grouped into three categories according to the time frame, reflecting their social and political backgrounds. The early seventeenth century was when the Tokugawa *bakufu* came to power and endeavored to firmly establish its authority with strict control across the country. The shogunate ordered daimyo to leave their wives and children resident in Edo as political hostages. There are accounts of these women's travel to Edo, such as "*Azumaji no ki*" (My Journey to the East) in 1600 by Maeda Matsuko, the wife of Maeda Toshiie, the founder of Kaga domain, and "*Michi no ki*" (A Journal of My Travel) in 1633 by Tokugawa

Haru, the wife of Tokugawa Yoshinao, the founder of Owari domain. They each departed strongly resolved, as indicated in "*Azumaji no ki,*" "What on earth reason would I have to complain? This is my duty for my lord, for the good of the world, and more than anything for my beloved son." The author, at the same time, expresses her longing for home, the loneliness of the journey, and anxiety about life in Edo.

The eighteenth century started with the flourishing of Genroku culture[94] and saw the further spread of National studies (*kokugaku*).[95] Around the scholars of National studies, who often taught *waka* as well, congregated a group of women poets. They began to travel searching for experience and poetic inspiration, and composed travel diaries with verses of *waka* included. Women of the daimyo class were no exception, although their recreational outings were normally limited to the areas east of Hakone *sekisho*. Among their accounts of such travel are "*Ishihara-ki*" (Journal of Our Days in Ishihara) in 1717 and "*Kotonohagusa*" (Leaves of Words) in 1730 ca. by Kuroda Tosako, the wife of Kuroda Naokuni, the Shimodate daimyo in Hitachi province; "*Yayoi no tabi*" (A Journey in Third Month) in 1777 by Hosokawa Noriko, the wife of Hosokawa Okisato, daimyo of Kumamoto's subordinate domain Udo in Higo province; "*Minobu kikō*" (A Journey to Minobu) in 1789 by Satake Hisa, the daughter of Satake Yoshimine, the Akita daimyo in Dewa province; and "*Tabi nikki*" (Travel Diary) in 1821 by Tozawa Mizuko, the wife of Tozawa Masachika, the Shinshō daimyo in Dewa province. "*Ikaho-ki*" (Ikaho Diary) by Nakagawa Man, the wife of Nakagawa Hisamori, the Oka daimyo in Bungo province, may be categorized with this group, although it was written substantially earlier, in 1639.

Some diaries were written by widows, who traveled home from Edo to their late husbands' domains; among which are "*Azuma no yume*" (Dreams of the East) in 1669 by Kōsei-in of the Sadowara daimyo Shimazu Hisataka, "*Umibe no akiiro*" (Autumn Colors on the Shore) in 1782 by Hosokawa Noriko mentioned above, and "*Koshi no yamafumi*" (Passing the Hills of Koshi)[96] in 1838 by Maeda Takako, widow of the Kaga daimyo Maeda Tadahiro.

The nineteenth century was a turbulent era, when the *bakufu* faced an unprecedented crisis for its very existence. Unlike for commoners, it was out of the question for women of the privileged but highly restricted daimyo class to travel for political activities of their own choosing. They did travel, however, tossed about by shifting political winds, including the relaxation of the alternate attendance system in 1862. Many such journeys were recorded during the closing years of the Tokugawa period; in particular, a relatively large number were written by daimyo wives of the western regions, who traveled between Edo and their home domains. Among them are "*Gekoku nikki*" (The Voyage Home) in 1863 by Matsudaira Shigeko, the wife of Matsudaira Chikayoshi of Kitsuki domain in Bungo province; "*Haru no yamamichi*" (Springtime Mountain Road) in 1863 by Arima Haruko, the wife of Arima Yoritō of Kurume domain in Chikugo province; "*Gojū-san tsugi nemuri no ai no te*" (Napping along the Fifty-Three Post Stations) in 1863 and "*Kairiku kaerizaki kotoba no tebyōshi*" (Rhythmic Songs for the Voyage Home) in 1865, both by Jūshin-in Mitsuko, the wife of Naitō Masayori of Nobeoka domain in Hyūga province; "*Edokudari nikki*" (Leaving Edo) in 1863 by Shimazu Yoriko, the wife of Shimazu Tadayuki of Sadowara domain in Hyūga province; and "*Matsu no shizuku*" (Dew Drops on Pine Trees), an account of an evacuation to her natal home in Saga domain in 1868 by Matsudaira Takeko, the wife of Matsudaira Naoyoshi of Kawagoe domain in Musashi province.

The Boshin War involved not only the families of commoners and retainers but those of the daimyo class as well. Driven out of their castles and provinces, aristocratic women, too, recorded their lives in exile. They wrote while desperately trying to survive the fierce battles of 1868. Among their diaries are "*Michi no ki*" (A Record of the Journey) by Niwa Hisako, the wife of Niwa Nagakuni of Nihonmatsu domain in Mutsu province; "*Nagaoka rakujō yori Aizu Sendai made no nikki*" (Fall of Nagaoka Castle and Journey to Aizu and Sendai) by Makino Tsuneko, the wife of Makino Tadakuni of Nagaoka domain in Echigo province; and "*Takiya no ki*" (Takiya Diary) by Hori Yūko, the wife of Hori Naoyasu of Muramatsu domain in Echigo province.

Now let us examine some of those diaries written in different eras under the Tokugawa rulers.

Journey to Edo as Hostage

In the eighth month of 1634 during the reign of the third shogun, Iemitsu, the *bakufu* extended the application of alternate attendance to those in hereditary vassalage to the Tokugawa (*fudai daimyo*)[97] as well; that is, they, too, were required to move their wives and children to Edo. The system had its precedent in the preceding era; the then-ruler Toyotomi Hideyoshi[98] situated daimyo mansions in the areas surrounding his castles in Osaka and Fushimi, forcing their masters to shuttle between their home provinces and the capital, where their wives and children were compelled to remain. Ieyasu, having assumed the position of shogun in 1603, followed Hideyoshi's example. He strongly promoted that *tozama* "outside" daimyo[99] attend Edo in alternating years while their wives and children reside in the shogun's capital permanently. As early as 1605, Tōdō Takatora, the Tsu daimyo in Ise province, transferred his wife Shōju-in and son Takatsugu to his Edo mansion. Asano Yukinaga of Wakayama in Kishū province and Date Masamune of Sendai in Mutsu province followed suit soon after.

Among them was the first woman who moved to Edo as a true hostage. At Ieyasu's request fifty-four-year-old Hōshun-in, wife of Maeda Toshiie[100] of Kanazawa, left Fushimi in the fifth month of 1600 for the long journey to Edo. She intended to prove the innocence of her son Toshinaga, who had been accused of plotting a rebellion against the Tokugawa before the Battle of Sekigahara. The diary *"Azumaji no ki"* (My Journey to the East) was apparently written by Hōshun-in's lady-in-waiting, who accompanied her mistress to Edo. The narrative sympathetically relates the loneliness of the trip.

> We bade farewell to our loved ones. Whether leaving or staying, there was no difference in the depth of grief. We repeatedly looked back at the mountains of Kyoto, which were disappearing from our sight gradually. What a forlorn journey it was.

Even the famous sights along the Tōkaidō could not hearten Hōshun-in, who found pathos in everything she saw around her. The long summer rains slowed their journey and raindrops hit the windows with a depressing sound. After passing the mountains of Hakone, where the *sekisho* was yet to be erected, the party at last arrived in Edo. Though Ieyasu received her with great respect and deference, Hōshun-in could hardly feel at home in the strange land of Edo. Anything she saw, be it morning clouds or the evening moon, vividly reminded her of Kyoto, her home. For many days she would often sit up in bed throughout the night remembering the lonely journey from home.

One of Ieyasu's sons, Tokugawa Yoshinao of Nagoya, was also among the daimyo who sent their wives to Edo. The thirty-one-year-old Kōgen-in Haru left Nagoya for Edo in 1633.4. Her diary *"Michi no ki"* (A Journal of My Travel) includes some twenty verses of *waka*. She diligently recorded the names of the places she passed and composed poems referring to, and inspired by, classical *waka* poems and traditions related to those places. Thus focusing her mind on literary creation, Kōgen-in tried to forget the melancholy of traveling far from home.

> In traveling clothes—
> awakened to the loneliness of journey
> on a sleepless night,
> do I hear a dog barking loudly
> as if to intensify my melancholy
>
> All I can do
> is to sail across the floating world
> like a small boat—
> appearing and disappearing on the
> surface of the rapid stream of water

Traveling east—
is it real or a dream,
I cross the ridge of
the mountain of Uzu, walking
down the narrow ivy-covered paths

Longing for the people
at home, I cannot help but
write to them,
asking them, "Do you see the
same clouds in the gloomy sky?"

Many women of daimyo families must have shared these sentiments, making the same lonely journey one after another during the following years.

Excursions of a Daimyo Wife

Immigration of daimyo wives to the shogun's capital diminished in frequency as time went by, as increasing numbers of their children were being born in the Edo residences. The lives of daimyo wives in Edo, though they were often described as 'hostages,' apparently afforded more freedom than expected. They could go to town with few restrictions and even travel freely, as long as the destinations were not beyond Hakone and the other *sekisho* barriers surrounding the Kantō region. Excursions to nearby places, such as Kamakura and Enoshima, and hot spring tours to Ikaho are recorded in several diaries.

The diary entitled "*Ishihara-ki*" (Journal of Our Days in Ishihara) by Kuroda Tosako, the wife of the Shimodate daimyo, is one of those works. Their primary residence in Edo was lost in the great fire that broke out in the first month of 1717, forcing the Kurodas to move to their secondary house[101] in Honjo-Ishihara. There, the family lived for a year and nine months until their main mansion in Tokiwabashi was rebuilt, and Tosako, then about thirty-seven years old, recorded the peaceful days with her husband Naokuni and their three daughters.

Perhaps inspired by the lightheartedness emerging from their temporary residence, Tosako would go out four or five times a month on average. Those outings naturally included various duties as the matron of the family, especially while her husband was absent from Edo in alternating years. She also had obligations to the Yanagisawa family, the lord of Kōfu domain; Tosako had been officially adopted as the late Yanagisawa Yoshiyasu's[102] daughter as a formal step to marry into the Kuroda family. In addition to attending annual events and services with the both families, Tosako obviously found enough time to enjoy outings with her daughters, and occasionally with her husband and attendants, too.

She frequented various temples to pray for the happiness of the family.
She also enjoyed seasonal events and the beauty of nature: viewing cherry
blossoms in Ueno, wisteria blossoms in a Kameido shrine, rice planting in
a nearby village, and fireworks at Ryōgoku. Her activities included sailing
down the Sumida River, strolling around the fields while picking herbs and
flowers, and so on. The family would make a tour of temples on religious
holidays, throw flower viewing parties with *sake* and delicacies, and at times
they were in turn feted by their hosts at the places they visited, sometimes
coming home late at night, around eleven or midnight.

During their temporary residence at Ishihara, their daughter Toyoko married. On the eighteenth day of the twelfth month, Tosako stayed home after
sending off the bride's procession, while quietly reflecting upon her loneliness mixed with the feeling of relief.

> My daughter, who I thought was just a child until yesterday, has grown up be-
> fore I knew, and has now left me as a bride. I am full of pride and happiness,
> though lonely to have to let go of the girl who stayed by my side all these years.
> I have taught her the knowledge and wisdom to manage the household and sent
> her off to her journey as a bride.

Now, Tosako had a new destination for her outings. Soon after New Year's
Day, she called on her daughter at the Matsudairas, the family Toyoko had
married into. She visited her again in the fourth month; this time the mother
stayed there for five days, upon the invitation of her son-in-law Matsudaira
Tadaakira. The absence of her husband Naokuni, now on duty in his home
province, was also an incentive for her to accept the invitation. When Toyoko
came back to her parents' house for a three-day visit, the mother frequently
took her out to entertain her.

As soon as she received the news of her daughter's safe delivery of a baby,
the elated Tosako hurried to see Toyoko. That her first grandchild was a boy
doubled her joy. Her prayers at various temples and shrines must have been
answered, she thought. She was totally absorbed in her role as caretaker for
Toyoko and her newborn baby, and ended up staying at her daughter's place
for twenty-three days.

Her diary reveals that Tosako's sentiments as a mother were no different
from those of commoner women, though certainly she was better off financially and had more free time at her disposal. It seems that she would often
decide to go out on the spur of the moment, inspired by good weather, for
instance. But Tosako's active lifestyle was obviously not inspired only by the
circumstances of the family's temporary residence. She was quite an active
woman by nature, which can be inferred from "*Kotonohagusa*" (Leaves of
Words), another diary that she began writing at the age of fifty-four.

After being widowed, Tosako continued to manage the house as its mistress, assisted by her adopted son Naozumi, conducting memorial services for the ancestors, socializing with relatives, maintaining close contacts with the family temple, etc. These responsibilities did not prevent her from spending time with her grandchildren; she was even present at her granddaughter's childbirth and stayed for many days to take care of her. She was indeed an obliging and active grandmother.

Return Trip to a Husband's Fief

In 1862, towards the end of the Tokugawa period, both Edo and Kyoto were in the midst of political turmoil and social unrest. In the first month, clansmen of Mito domain attacked and injured Andō Nobumasa, the chief of the Shogun's Council of Elders, just outside Edo Castle. Around that time in Kyoto, too, were there frequent attacks and assassinations of Imperial loyalists. In the second month, Imperial princess Kazunomiya wed the fourteenth shogun Iemochi at Edo Castle. In the eighth month, the *bakufu* eased the alternate attendance system and issued permission for daimyo wives and children to leave Edo to return to their home provinces. In reality, the proclamation was more of an order, rather than permission, for evacuation from the tumultuous capital of the *bakufu*.

Edo had by that time long been home to most daimyo wives and children. It was not easy for them to leave the city, where they had lived comfortably almost their entire lives. Jūshin-in, the wife of Naitō Masayori, the former Nobeoka daimyo in Hyūga province, was among those affected. "Never having left Edo until my advanced age, I feel depressed just to think of a long journey to the far west. Can't I find some excuse to postpone the date of my departure?" lamented the sixty-three-year-old matron. She seriously considered remaining in Edo, but persuaded by her family and friends, finally left the shogun's capital in tears on a rainy day at the beginning of the fourth month of 1863.

The party traveled along the Tōkaidō, carrying their mistress in a palanquin. At a stopover in Hakone, Jūshin-in was able to relax in a hot bath at an inn called Fukuzumi. The inn's beautifully furnished interior, well-tended garden, water drawn from the hot springs, and the delicacies served for the guests all turned out to be quite satisfying, which inspired Jūshin-in to take up her favorite brush; she drew not only a complete view of the inn with mountains in its background but its floor plan, furniture and the layout of the garden as well. Passing the *sekisho* without incident, their journey continued smoothly.

Regaining her cheerful demeanor, Jūshin-in busily kept a journal, with vivid descriptions of various inconveniencies she encountered every day. For example, she became so accustomed to being on the road that she even learned to take a nap in her palanquin, though she hit the back of her head every time it shook while she slept. "I have a bump on the back of my head, and it hurts quite a bit. It's not very seemly but I don't know what to do," she wrote. Her experiences naturally included a few disappointments, too, such as when she could not see Mt. Fuji clearly due to her deteriorating eyesight. On another occasion, she tried walking for a change, as recommended by her attendants, through a grove of pine trees, but found it rather boring and returned to her palanquin shortly. The chestnut rice cake, a specialty of Iwabuchi in Shizuoka did not interest her, either. "Nothing special," was her dismissive comment on the confectionary. What interested her most were clearly the architecture, floor plans, and garden arrangements of the places she visited, which she laboriously recorded in her drawings.

The warm hospitality she encountered throughout her journey erased her melancholy and reawakened her abundant curiosity towards everything around her. At the *honjin* in Kakegawa, messengers came from the Ōta clan, the domain lord, to present a *kasutera* sponge cake[103] to Jūshin-in with formal words of greeting attached.

In Hamamatsu, they found the *honjin* quite crowded, accommodating four other parties of daimyo wives. The inn master advised that they had better cross the lake early in the morning to Arai *sekisho*, so Jūshin-in and her attendants left the inn before dawn, lanterns in hand. They crossed the lake in a red lacquer-painted houseboat with a special curtain spread across its side. But for its return trip after dropping off Jūshin-in's party at Arai, the crew swiftly dismantled the roof and the cedar doors, and tucked them in the bottom of the boat. "What a quick, efficient, and thoughtful arrangement!" Jūshin-in observed in amazement. After the formalities imposed by the Inspector of Women at Arai *sekisho*,[104] the party arrived at the *honjin*, where they enjoyed lunch, which included *sake*, eel, and sweets.

The ferryboat to Kuwana was specially prepared for them by the Tokugawa branch family of Nagoya domain. It carried banners and had a white crepe curtain spread with the Tokugawa crest dyed on it. An arabesque patterned indigo blue awning covered the boat's tower. The picturesque vessel, called *Shiratorimaru*, normally for the shogun's official use on visits to Kyoto, was there to ferry Jūshin-in and her party across the river, an expression of goodwill towards the Naito clan, relations of the Tokugawa.[105] The interior of the boat was carefully decorated and the tugboat proceeded ceremoniously accompanied by drumbeats and sailors' songs. In the midst of many spectators the boat was moored right by the garden of the *honjin*.

They crossed Mt. Suzuka, which was higher than they had expected, crossed the Seta Bridge (*Seta no karahashi*)[106] on foot, and arrived at Ishiyama-dera.[107] At this famous temple Jūshin-in was excited to view a portrait of the author Murasaki Shikibu, her ink stone, and her handwritten sutra. The visit to the temple meant a great deal to Jūshin-in, who had not only copied, but also annotated all fifty-four chapters of *The Tale of Genji*. They rested overnight at Fushimi near Kyoto, and then headed for Osaka. Crossing a river on the way she called over the famous boat peddlers, known by the nickname "eat-eat boats," to buy some food and *sake*. The peddlers were very pushy, yelling "eat, eat" in an accent that sounded vulgar to her ears. The rice cake she bought turned out to be inedible since it had cinders mixed in the sweetened beans to enhance its color. Jūshin-in was very angry but her anger did not last long, as she started dozing off as usual.

In Osaka, she visited a teahouse, accompanied by a maid. There, Jūshin-in tried to teach a parlor game called *kitsune-ken* (lit. "fox fist") to the proprietress, even volunteering to demonstrate its dance as well. But the proprietress could not say "*kitsune*" accurately, and would pronounce the word "*ketsune*" instead with an Osaka accent no matter how many times Jūshin-in demonstrated. Finally, they both burst out laughing. She went on to visit other teahouses and restaurants, and again requested dance and *shamisen* music. "Neither *taiko* drums nor hand drums here sound lively—quite dull and monotonous!" On a sightseeing excursion to a brothel in a licensed quarter,[108] the courtesans "appeared unsophisticated and the guys were not dashing either." Overall, she did not seem to have favorable impressions of the commoners in Osaka. In addition, the daimyo wife's palanquin would attract a number of onlookers; some were audacious enough to peek inside and report to each other "a monk, a monk" referring to Jūshin-in's shaved head. However, the fact that Jūshin-in was able to go out and enjoy the city, in spite of her status as a daimyo wife, probably owed greatly to Osaka's open atmosphere at the time.[109]

From Osaka, they traveled across the Seto Inland Sea by boat. On their way, they stopped to pay a visit to Konpira Shrine, having their skipper help bear her palanquin. "Even blind people, if they have strong faith, climb up the hill to the shrine. How could I possibly pass by it without offering my prayers," thus determined, Jūshin-in climbed the hundreds of stone steps gasping and panting, and finally made her visit to the shrine.

At the port were vessels of various daimyo families moored due to the rainy weather, to which entertainers approached to offer their services. The cheerful sounds of drums and *shamisen* leaking from some of the boats consoled the exhausted mind and body of Jūshin-in, who was a great fan of music. There were also women who approached the boats, carrying a large tray with fishes on their heads, loudly calling out "Won't you buy fish?" Some of them rowed small boats by themselves.

During another port call at Mitsukue in Iyo province, Jūshin-in went to the village headman's house to borrow their bath. At the port of Shimonae, to stave off boredom, she had her maid play the *shamisen* for her and began to practice dancing in the dimmed light, intending to perform it in front of her family once she arrived in Nobeoka. But Jūshin-in was embarrassed later to learn that, unbeknownst to her, she had had an audience that night; local officials had quietly approached in a small boat and were watching her dance lesson through the window.

When she left Edo, Jūshin-in wrote, "I am already over sixty, and yet I am not allowed to stay in the house in this eastern capital, where I have lived all these years and to which I am so accustomed and attached. What a harsh world has it become! I cannot stop the tears streaming down my cheeks." But this curious, multi-talented woman was never beaten by boredom no matter what her situation, and soon she began to actively enjoy her travel. She made her daily experiences full of excitement, spreading laughter to the people around her, and completed her fifty-five-day journey home to Nobeoka safe and sound on the second day of the sixth month, accompanied by her granddaughter Mitsu.

Once on the road, Jūshin-in no longer cried nor desperately longed for Edo but began to devote her full attention to the scenery and the lives of the people she encountered. She grasped and described things straightforwardly, sometimes even critically. Her main interests definitely concerned architecture, floor plans, furniture, gardens, shapes of boats, hair ornaments, and the like, which she observed accurately and humorously. Her diary, entitled "*Gojū-san tsugi nemuri no ai no te*" (Napping along the Fifty-Three Post Stations), includes about fifty ink paintings and drawings, characterized by her powerful brushstrokes. Her diary vividly conveys the atmosphere of the time and place.

Jūshin-in had resigned herself to the likelihood that never again would she be able to see Edo, but two years later, an opportunity arose to travel back to the eastern capital. She again kept a diary of the seventy-two-day journey, expressing her elated state of mind in its title "*Kairiku kaerizaki kotoba no tebyōshi*" (Rhythmic Songs for the Voyage Home). The preface of the diary, with its rhythmic style, fully describes her happiness on the occasion:[110]

> So light-hearted am I, and so cheerful is the accompaniment, in tune with this season of cherry blossoms. Is it a dream or reality? A balmy spring day it is. Under the shade of a willow tree do I nap a short while, but it is hard to awaken in a rocking palanquin. The pine groves are deep green along the Sea of Akashi. I don't recall Naniwazu,[111] though am familiar with Tokiwazu.[112] Now I will write my diary, but to the accompaniment of my favorite melodies from Edo. How thrilling it will be . . .

Fall of a Castle and Exile

Negotiations at Ojiya (in Niigata) between the army general Kawai Tsugunosuke of Nagaoka domain and Iwamura Seiichirō of the Imperial army broke down; the former's petition for halting the attack and discontinuing the war was dismissed. Nagaoka domain immediately joined the League of Ōu Major Domains to fight against the new Imperial government.

> At around eight o'clock in the morning on the nineteenth day of the fifth month of 1868, a year of the dragon, Nagaoka Castle fell. Still in my nightwear, with no palanquin available, I fled from the garden gate, wearing a woven hat and straw sandals. The enemy had already approached close by, shooting bullets here and there. Luckily I left the castle uninjured. . . .

Nagaoka Castle fell quickly after a surprise attack early on the morning of 5.19. Tsune, the twenty-five-year-old wife of daimyo Makino Tadakuni, fled the castle, sought shelter in a farmer's house, where she was provided with a meal, and then ran away in the rain into the mountains. With no male attendant available to her, Tsune climbed the long, steep "eighty *ri* pass"[113] on foot, braving a heavy rain. On top of the mountain she spread oil paper and lay down on it with her sister Fusa. As the night wore on, though the rain had let up, her face was wet and the cold pierced her nightwear-clad body. Her maid stayed up all night to keep the fire. Still having nothing to eat the following day, they drank clear spring water to stave off hunger. At night they at last found their way to Tadamimura in the territory of Aizu, where the women were given one night accommodation at a farmer's house. Her feet were swollen and extremely painful, rendering Tsune unable to walk without help. The following day the women went to Kenpuku-ji in palanquins provided by the authorities of Aizu domain. There, Tsune was reunited with her father, who was the former daimyo, and his other children. They lived together at the temple for a few months, and on 7.24 received the good news that their army had recaptured Nagaoka Castle. But their joy did not last long; five days later an express messenger arrived to report that the castle had again fallen to the Imperial army.

Before long, the castle town of Aizu was crowded with refugees from Nagaoka. The retainers' families and those who were injured in the fall of the castle were heading for Aizu, where their lord had evacuated.

As the enemy swarmed towards Aizu Castle, Tsune's family left the temple at midnight on 8.22 and continued their journey of escape for three days and three nights until they finally found an empty peasant house. Searching the house, the retainers found rice and some pickled foods in a corner of the kitchen, with which the party prepared a meal to stave off their hunger somewhat. They trudged further into the mountains, heading for Yonezawa. At one point they were told the enemy was drawing near. While the retainers loaded guns, Tsune resigned herself that she was at her end, but then was greatly relieved to learn that it had been a false report. Constantly exposed to danger, she could not help but wonder, "What on earth have I done to deserve such a horrifying existence?"

Nearing Yonezawa, they found a number of *sekisho* erected here and there, making their passage extremely difficult, and eventually they were told to turn back and go home. At one checkpoint the party was made to wait. While eating the rice balls offered to them, "talking about refugees of ancient times, and lamenting over our own fate with tears," one of the retainers patiently negotiated with the officials and finally obtained permission to pass in the evening.

Rejected by Yonezawa domain, they headed for Sendai. They staggered along the sawyer's road and fearfully crossed many suspension bridges covered with wisteria vines across the horrifyingly deep ravines, rough waters swirling at the bottom.

On 9.8, after a dangerous, frightening journey of some fifteen days, they arrived in Sendai and finally settled into a temple assigned to be their lodging. They remained there for about two months. After the war ended, they departed for Nagaoka on 11.9. The return trip was free of the terror of war, and though challenged by the snowy, mountainous roads, the party could occasionally appreciate beautiful views along the way.

On 11.28, they ended their six-month journey as refugees and came home to Nagaoka. Tsune wrote, "It is still hard to believe that we really traveled as far as Ōshū. It feels as if I was just having a long dream." She added three verses of *waka* at the end of her diary and a one-line foreword:

I composed the following poems at the departure of a certain lord for the east.

> Gathering clouds—
> cloud the heaven as you wish,
> Someday will we see
> the moment when all the clouds are
> cleared from our clouded minds

> Those who punish
> and those who are punished,
> Could there be any
> difference between their loyalties
> towards their beloved countries

> Melancholy or joyousness,
> whichever the heaven may bring to us,
> have we not to
> lament over our destiny
> should we still be alive together

"A certain lord" in her foreword implicitly refers to her husband Tadakuni, who had originally come from Miyazu domain of Tango province to marry into the Makino family. After the war, Tadakuni subjected himself to voluntary confinement at the Shōei-ji temple in Tokyo to express his fealty to the new government. Tsune wrote a diary of her days of exile and sent it with the above *waka* verses to Tadakuni, writing in a note that it was "just a humble account of the journey which I composed for your distraction." In the second month of the following year, twenty thousand *koku* was endowed to her stepbrother Tadakatsu, and Nagaoka domain was restored.

In any historical era wars would break out between lords, forcing women and commoners to flee from the gunfire and into miserable lives as refugees, often losing loved ones during their travails. Many women diligently recorded how ordinary people struggled in those circumstances. Their writings are a true legacy for posterity.

NOTES

1. More works have been added to her collection since, and the number has reached well over two hundred as of 2010. Shiba Keiko, Letter to the translator, p. 5.

2. Strictly speaking, according to Shiba (Letter to the translator, p. 2), women of the Tokugawa period did not have surnames; in the case of artists, especially painters, they would often sign their names as such-and-such (first names) of so-and-so clan (natal family names). At the same time, however, Shiba points out, based on her research, that it was not unusual for women, once married, to use their husbands' surnames. In her original text of this book, Shiba normally introduces the female author as in the following: her first name, with her status as the wife/daughter of so-and-so (the full name of her husband/father), especially those of the samurai class. In my translation, I adopt the modern custom for convenience, writing her full name, with surname first (either maiden or husband's) followed by personal name. A woman who has taken Buddhist vows is normally addressed by her Buddhist name.

3. Ise Grand Shrine (*Ise jingū*) is located in Ise City, Mie prefecture. It consists of the Outer Shrine and Inner Shrine; the Inner Shrine enshrines the Sun Goddess (*Amaterasu ōmikami*), the central figure of Japanese mythology, as its main deity. Ise Shrine, therefore, is revered as the holiest of all Shinto shrines in Japan. Its origin is narrated in old literature, including in *Records of Ancient Matters* (*Kojiki*) and *The Chronicles of Japan* (*Nihon shoki*).

4. Tōkaidō, connecting Edo and Kyoto, was the greatest and most-traveled route among the five highways (*Gokaidō*) that the Tokugawa government established by developing existing roads. The other four were the Nakasendō, Kōshū-kaidō, Ōshū-kaidō, and Nikko-kaidō, according to *Fukutake kogo jiten*, ed. Inoue Muneo and Nakamura Yukihiro (Fukutake Shoten, 1988), pp. 1386–87. A comprehensive study of traffic infrastructure at the time is available in Constantine Nomikos Vaporis, *Breaking Barriers: Travel and the State in Early Modern Japan* (Cambridge: Council on East Asian Studies, Harvard University, 1994). According to Vaporis, the latter three are called the Kōshū-dōchū, Ōshū-dōchū, and Nikko-dōchū. p. 19.

5. The mountain, with an altitude of 866 meters and located in Shizuoka prefecture, is also called Mt. Akiba. Akiba Shrine, which is considered to have its origin in

mountain worship, later was heavily influenced by Buddhist thought and developed as a spiritual site for mountaineering asceticism. The shrine received support from the Tokugawa and prospered during the early modern period, but was discontinued in the Meiji period as a result of the separation of Shinto and Buddhism. See Shirai Eiji and Toki Masanori, eds., *Jinja jiten* (Tōkyōdō Shuppan, 2004), p. 7.

6. The temple is situated near the peak of Mt. Hōraiji in Aichi prefecture. It has a *tōshōgū* (a shrine that enshrines Tokugawa Ieyasu) in its precinct, according to Tanioka Takeo, ed., *Nihon chimei jiten* (Sanseidō, 2007), p. 1104, indicating a strong connection with the Tokugawa. In Japanese, the names of Buddhist temples typically end with either —*ji* or —*dera* (both meaning temple).

7. Genji (the Minamoto clan) and Heike (the Taira clan) were rival warriors in the 12th century; the Heike came to power first and flourished for a few decades but was completely defeated by the Genji at the Battle of Dannoura in 1185. *Tale of the Heike* (*Heike monogatari*) is a narration of the rise and fall of Heike; the tale has a number of famous episodes, which were later adapted into and popularized by various forms of art and literature, including *nō, kabuki, bunraku*, and popular novels.

8. Smallest of the four main islands of the Japanese archipelago, it lies southwest of Osaka.

9. The shrine, located in Kagawa prefecture in Shikoku, was originally called Koto-hira Shrine, but later acquired the name Konpira (originally, the Sanskrit 'Kumbhira') due to *shinbutsu konkō* (lit. mixture of Shinto and Buddhism), a kind of syncretism that combines the ways of Buddha and Shinto. Konpira worship became very popular, especially during the late Tokugawa period, when the number of worshipers at Konpira was second only to that of Ise Shrine. Shirai and Toki, eds., *Jinja jiten*, pp. 144–145.

10. Since ancient times the Seto Inland Sea (*Setonaikai*) has been a major sea route to and from the Kansai region, where the old capitals Nara and Kyoto, and other large cities such as Osaka and Sakai were located. There is a body of literary works that utilize the voyage across the Seto Inland Sea as important motifs, according to Maeda, a tradition that goes back to *waka* poems in the fifteenth volume of *Man'yōshū*, which includes poems by Japanese envoys to Silla (an ancient nation in the Korean Penin-sula) from the 8th century. See Maeda Yoshi, *Edo jidai joryū bungeishi—tabi nikki hen* (Kasama Shoin, 1998), p. 83.

11. *Waka* refers to traditional Japanese poetry, often synonymous with its major form *tanka*, the thirty-one syllable verse, although it may include the longer, but mi-nor, form *chōka* and now obsolete *sedōka*. In this book, too, *waka* refers to *tanka*. In my translation I present each poem in five lines, indicating that the original Japanese verse has the five-seven-five-seven-seven syllabic rhythm.

12. Forty-seven samurai, former retainers of the late Akō daimyo Asano Naga-nori (Takumi-no-kami), raided the mansion of Kira Yoshinaka (Kōzuke-no-suke) on 1702.12.4 and killed him, avenging their lord's death. Although vengeance was prohibited under Tokugawa law, the forty-seven samurai's loyalty to their late lord holds the power to move people; the story was later adapted into *kabuki* and *bunraku* (puppet theater) plays.

13. Head of the Heike clan (see note 7), he came to power after the Heiji War in 1159.

14. The resort is located in present-day Gunma prefecture, northwest of Tokyo. The water there is known for its good quality.

15. He died before his mother, fourteen years after their journey. Engyo kept on encouraging his literary-minded mother to write an account of their travel, and he himself made various notes during their journey, apparently for his mother to use as reference. Maeda Yoshi, *Kinsei nyonin no tabinikki shū* (Fukuoka: Ashi Shobō, 2001), p. 140.

16. Apparently her given name was Tsugi, but it was customary to add —*jo* (meaning 'woman') at the end of a woman's name as a courtesy; except the names with the *ko* ending, such as Nakako, Shigako, Ayako.

17. The temple, located in Nagano prefecture, was founded in 602. It has always drawn faithful visiting from all over Japan, irrespective of the sects they themselves followed.

18. Bandō is equivalent to the Kantō region.

19. Kikusha-ni was her Buddhist name, acquired when she took holy vows; it means "a nun at a chrysanthemum hut" (*Kikusha*=chrysanthemum hut) and (*ni*=nun). She was born in 1753, her given name Michi, the oldest daughter of a samurai of the Chōfu domain, and married into a farmer's family at the age of 16, according to Kado Reiko, *Edo joryūbungaku no hakken*, p. 321.

20. The seventeen-syllable verse was simply called *ku* at that time. The first unit (the *hokku*) of the humorous linked verses (*haikai*) came to be appreciated independently as well during the Edo period, but the term *haiku* was not coined until the late 19th century during the Meiji period. In this book, I present the English translation of each *ku* in three lines, indicating that the original *ku* is in the five-seven-five syllabic rhythm.

21. It was not uncommon for both men and women to take Buddhist vows without particularly strong religious inclinations, but rather as a rite of passage, and remain outside the monasteries or convents and live among lay people.

22. It was, and is, a common practice for a *haikai/haiku* poet to acquire a pen name which indicates the poet's artistic inclination. Here, his name can be interpreted as follows: *Chōboen* "in the garden from dawn to dusk" and *Sankyō* "wearing a hat of poetic madness."

23. This genre of literature had existed for a long time but reached the height of its popularity during the Edo period. Usually it referred to nonstandard, comic *renga* (linked verse) and "was first an amusement (as renga had also been) but it took on seriousness with the evolution of the *Teimon*, *Danrinfū* and *Shōfū*, the first associated with Matsunaga Teitoku, the second with Nishiyama Sōin, and the last with Matsuo Bashō." Earl Miner, Hiroko Odagiri, and Robert E. Morrell, eds., *The Princeton Companion to Classical Japanese Literature* (Princeton: Princeton University Press, 1985), p. 276.

24. A comprehensive study of the art of Matsuo Bashō (1644–94) is found in Shirane Haruo, *Traces of Dreams: Landscape, Cultural Memory, and the Poetry of Bashō* (Stanford: Stanford University Press, 1998). Bashō, in his later creative years, spent a substantial amount of time traveling, seeking poetic inspiration and further refinements of the *haikai* spirit. Among his literary accounts of journeys,

Oku no hosomichi (*Narrow Road to the Interior*) is probably best known and most widely read; it is an account of a five-month journey to Michinoku (the northern part of Honshū, the largest of the Japanese four main islands).

25. The southernmost main island of Japan.

26. Yoshino is a site renowned for cherry blossoms; therefore the two images are intimately associated in literary convention.

27. Saigyō was born into a samurai family in 1118, but at the age of twenty-three he took Buddhist tonsure and spent the rest of his life traveling and composing *waka*. Saigyō loved cherry blossoms and composed many poems on the flower.

28. Pale pink cherry blossoms in the distance are often compared to images of clouds and spring mists, a conventional *waka* technique called "*mitate* (visual allusion)."

29. *Haikai* is a form of literature that is inherently communal, as is thoroughly explicated in Shirane, *Traces of Dreams*. At a *haikai* gathering the main guest typically composes a first verse complimenting the host and his surroundings. The poet sometimes rendered the verse in calligraphy accompanied by a suitable quick drawing, and presented it to the host as a gift. Kikusha-ni's gestures at Tōkaidō post stations can be seen as emblematic of the spirit of a *haikai* poet.

30. The name of an office of the Imperial Court, not of the Tokugawa *bakufu*.

31. The name of an office of the Imperial Court.

32. While the administrative center Edo became the center of culture by the end of the Tokugawa period, Kyoto also maintained its status as the center of high culture created and preserved for centuries by the Imperial family and court nobles.

33. A cone-shaped, iron-colored cup, which was used at a Zen temple in Mt. Tian Mu in China. A Japanese monk, after studying in China, brought one back during the Kamakura period (1192–1333). Kindaichi Haruhiko and Ikeda Yasaburō, eds., *Gakken kokugo daijiten* (Gakushū Kenkyūsha, 1978), p. 1358.

34. Nanmei and his son Shōyō were both renowned scholars of *kobunjigaku*, a variant of Ancient Learning (*kogaku*) that was one of the two main varieties of Neo-Confucianism. The *bakufu*, however, approved the other variety, *shushigaku,* for the formal education of the sons of its retainers, and in 1790 banned teaching the other schools of Neo-Confucianism. Many daimyo followed suit; Nanmei was ordered into life-time confinement by the domain in 1792, probably because of this tide in academia, and his outspoken, independent-minded character was not helpful in such a political climate. See Machida Saburō, "*Kamei Nanmei, Shōyō*" in *Hakatagaku: Hakata chōnin to gakusha no mori*, ed. Asahi Shimbun Fukuoka Honbu (Fukuoka: Ashi Shobō, 1996), pp. 109–123.

35. During the Tokugawa period, all daimyo were to travel from their domains to Edo in alternating years to attend the shogun, while leaving their wives and daughters in Edo as political hostages. An in-depth study of the system is provided in Constantine Nomikos Vaporis, *Tour of Duty: Samurai, Military Service in Edo, and the Culture of Early Modern Japan* (Honolulu: University of Hawaiʻi Press, 2008).

36. The buildings in the temple compound, located in the ancient capital Nara, are world's oldest extant wooden structures. It is believed to have been built by Prince Shōtoku (Shōtoku taishi/Umayado no ōji) and Empress Suiko in the early to late 7th century.

37. Her given name was Michi, according to Kado, *Edo joryūbungaku no hakken*, p. 229, and Saihin was a pen name as a *kanshi* poet. Scholars and poets of Chinese classics customarily acquire Sino-Japanese *noms de plume*, typically written as two *kanji* characters with Sino-Japanese pronunciation. The names of Confucian scholars and *kanshi* poets appearing in this book are all their Sino-Japanese pen names.

38. According to Miura Sueo, *Monogatari Akizuki shi* (Akizuki: Akizuki Kyōdokan, 1972), the tall, attractive Saihin applied no makeup, and did not have her long hair done up like other women of the time but let it hang straight and wore a sword on her waist when traveling. Quoted in Kado, *Edo joryūbungaku no hakken*, p. 231.

39. It is not clear why Shōkin had her father write the poem for her on that occasion. Kado's study portrays Shōkin as an accomplished scholar-poet trained by her father since childhood. Her given name was Tomo, and Shōkin was her *nom de plume*. She was gifted in drawing and calligraphy as well. When she was fifteen, her father had an additional room built in his house as her study, naming it *Yōchō-kyū*. The word *yōchō* (meaning quiet and beautiful) was taken from the Chinese classic *Shi Jing*. Shōkin married her father's disciple, Raishu, at the age of nineteen. Kado, pp. 220–224.

40. It was not only Shōkin who tried to stop Saihin; Shōkin's father Shōyō and Rai San'yō also believed it too reckless a plan for a woman to travel alone to Edo. Kado, p. 232.

41. It was actually a compound word made up of five *kanji* characters, each referring to "east," "west," "south," "north," and "person" respectively.

42. The last stanza of the poem that her father gave her when she left for Edo for the first time reads, "One would not allow his daughter to return home without her having made her name." Kado, p. 231.

43. It probably was for the same reason as is mentioned previously in note 34.

44. Off Hiroshima in the Seto Inland Sea. It is famous for Itsukushima Shrine; the foot of the red buildings in the compound is covered by water at a high tide.

45. This will be discussed as a part of women's educational background in Chapter Three.

46. Seigan and his wife Kōran were both *kanshi* poets and associates of Ema Saikō, an accomplished poetess from the same region. Studies on Saikō and her poems are introduced in note 3 of the Translator's Introduction.

47. The daughter of Shinoda Kasai, a physician of Shimoda, Izu. Unpō's genius was apparent since childhood; she lectured the wife of the Tsu daimyo at the age of thirteen. She is perhaps more highly regarded as a Confucian scholar than a poet. Kado, pp. 263–266.

48. Apparently, Kimikazu is this fisherman's given name and Goseidō his *kanshi* pen name.

49. Kagoshima actually does not border with China, but its location (the southernmost part of Kyūshū) must certainly have impressed Kyoto people as a faraway hinterland.

50. Another name for Miyajima. See note 44.

51. Takanabe is in the southern part of Kyūshū, not far from Kagoshima; her journey to Ōsaka, therefore, traces approximately a reverse route to Saisho Atsuko's travel from Kyoto to Kagoshima.

52. Short for the *Kokin waka shū* (*A Collection of Ancient and Modern Poems*), the first imperially-sponsored anthology of *waka*, compiled in the early 10th century. It retained its status in the *waka* canon for centuries.

53. There are many places with the same name across the country, but this is one of the post-station towns on the Tōkaidō, located in present-day Aichi prefecture.

54. Akahito was an 8th-century court poet, who was especially gifted in description of natural scenery.

55. Literally meaning 'poem of mutual inquiry'; two poets exchange their thoughts and emotions via *waka*. Naturally many *sōmonka* are poems of romantic love, but the genre includes those exchanged between family members, friends, colleagues, etc.

56. According to Maeda, Gensai suffered an illness that caused him hearing problems when he was thirty; he thereafter led the life of a literati, letting his younger brother be the Ikeda family successor. Gensai was an erudite scholar, who first pursued Confucian studies but later shifted his focus to National studies and the composition of *waka*. When he heard of the talented young Kiyoi, it is said, Gensai wished her for his son Makoto's wife. Kiyoi, whose talent was respected and treasured by both her husband and father-in-law, had three sons with Makoto and socialized in Gensai's literary circle. Maeda, *Edojidai joryū bungeishi*, pp. 331–338.

57. Ii Naosuke, who assumed the position of the *bakufu*'s Great Counselor (*tairō*) in 1858.4, signed the U.S.-Japan Treaty of Amity and Trade without receiving the Emperor's approval. He purged those who opposed the treaty; the number of those punished reached over one hundred including court nobles, daimyo, activists, and scholars. Toki's domain lord Tokugawa Nariaki was in the opposition group and criticized Ii's dictatorial measures. Naramoto Shin'ya, ed., *Nihon no rekishi: Bakumatsu tte nan darō* (PHP, 1990), pp. 28–29.

58. A long poem, included in the genre of *waka*. See note 11.

59. The shrine also underwent syncretism with Buddhism, and in the medieval period it was particularly worshiped by devotees of mountain asceticism. The shrine-temple was offered land yielding 1000 *koku* by the Tokugawa *bakufu* in 1612. Shirai and Toki, eds., *Jinja jiten*, p. 247.

60. To the names of post-station towns along the highways were often attached the word —*juku* at the end, meaning 'post station,' such as Atsutajuku and Maisakajuku.

61. Official checkpoints established at fifty-three locations along the Five Highways. Two chapters "A Curious Institution" and "Permits and Passages" in Vaporis' *Breaking Barriers* (pp. 99–174) offer detailed studies of the *sekisho* and how they functioned during the Tokugawa period.

62. Fuwa-no-seki was an important checkpoint during the Nara period but was abandoned in 789. It was a spot of historical interest during the Edo period, and was sometimes depicted in poems. Tanioka, ed., *Nihon chimei jiten*, pp. 1092–93.

63. When women of the court or of the high-ranking samurai class took Buddhist vows, they customarily acquired a name with the suffix —*in*.

64. The northernmost main island of Japan.

65. The largest main island of Japan.

66. Here is a poetic technique called *kakekotoba* (pivot word), the same sound meaning two things; the "*shira*" in "*Shirakawa*" alludes to the "*shira*" in "*shirazu* (do not know)."

67. The poem was selected in the early 13th century for the imperially-sponsored collection *Shin kokin waka shū.* The verse reads as follows: *Michi no be ni / shimizu nagaruru / yanagikage / shibashitote koso / tachidomaritsuru,* which roughly translates as "On the roadside / clear water streams / under the willow shade / where I stopped / for a little while." Bashō, a devotee of Saigyō and his *waka* poetry, found the willow tree during his journey to the interior and composed a 17-syllable verse there. Toyama Susumu, ed., *Bashō bunshū,* no. 17, *Shinchō Nihon koten shūsei* (Shinchōsha, 1978), pp. 115–116.

68. A site famous as one of the three most beautiful pine-tree groves in Japan.

69. Sakai, a thriving commercial city facing Osaka Bay, was a *bakufu* territory (*tenryō*).

70. Also called Saya-no-Nakayama, the site was depicted in various works, both prose and poetry, including *Sarashina Diary, Tale of the Heike,* and *Kokinshū.*

71. The other name for Atsuta. Miya (meaning "shrine") in this case also refers to Atsuta Shrine.

72. Because she was the wife of the newly-appointed Sakai Magistrate, an important office in the Tokugawa administration. Shiba, *Edo-ki no onnatachi ga mita Tōkaidō,* no. 4, *Edo-ki hito bunko* (Katsura Bunko, 2002), p. 217.

73. Seki was named after the *sekisho* of Suzuka; it was one of the three strictest *sekisho* of ancient times, along with Ōsaka-no-Seki and Fuwa-no-Seki. Jizōin is a noted temple founded by the priest Ikkyū. Tanioka, *Nihon chimei jiten,* p. 677.

74. Present-day Akita prefecture in northern Japan.

75. Present-day Gunma prefecture, northwest of Tokyo.

76. *Kyōka* literally means "mad *waka.*" It is *waka* with a humorous or witty cast of language or thought, and word plays involving several meanings were especially popular. Miner and others, eds., *Princeton Companion,* p. 287. Composition of *kyōka* often required knowledge of classical *waka,* and therefore, it was mainly practiced by the samurai aristocracy and learned townspeople.

77. It is unlikely that the Yamadas were literally "poor"; the term *binbō-gami* is normally used in a humorous, self-deprecating way, which is the case here as well.

78. According to Vaporis, the Tokugawa government outlawed the practice of prostitution in 1660, except for the licensed quarters, but "[t]he bakufu's hard-line position soon softened, however, and commoner inns were allowed to keep two prostitutes each, although they were now designated as *meshimori onna,* or 'serving girls.'" Vaporis, *Breaking Barriers,* p. 81.

79. Both Murozumi and Kaminoseki are in present-day Yamaguchi prefecture, facing Kyūshū across the Inland Sea.

80. Both Koyase and Yamae are in present-day Fukuoka prefecture.

81. Coal was discovered in Kyūshū earlier than any other part of Japan; records show that they were already engaged in coal mining during the second half of the 15th century. Maeda, *Edojidai joryū bungeishi,* p. 79.

82. Born into a samurai family of the Chōshū domain. Shōin (1830–59) was brilliant since childhood, and grew up to be a progressive thinker. His thought profoundly influenced his followers, which included noted activists Takasugi Shinsaku, Kusaka Genzui, and Yoshida Nenma. Shōin was thirty years old when he was executed. Naramoto, *Nihon no rekishi*, pp. 42–43.

83. The Boshin War refers to the series of five battles at five locations at different times during 1868–69; 1868 was the year of the *boshin*/dragon.

84. Seeing Matsushima, Bashō wrote that he gave up composing a verse and tried to sleep, but that it was impossible to fall asleep after being so profoundly moved by the superb beauty. "*Oku no hosomichi*," in *Bashō bunshū*, ed., Toyama, p. 129.

85. In present-day Iwate prefecture, northeastern Honshū.

86. *Tatami* are rectangular straw mats, each roughly 1 meter by 2 meters, used to cover the entire floor of a traditional Japanese room. The size of a room is often described in terms of the total number of *tatami* mats used in its flooring.

87. Her name appears a number of times in Rebecca L. Copeland, *Lost Leaves: Women Writers of Meiji Japan* (Honolulu: University of Hawai'i Press, 2000), an insightful work on another under-studied area of Japanese literary history. In addition to the discussion of women writers and the readership of the Meiji era in general, the book features three authors; Miyake Kaho, Wakamatsu Shizuko, and Shimizu Shikin.

88. A unit to measure quantities of rice, one *koku*=180 liter or 5.119 U.S. bushels.

89. The idea of the rickshaw was conceived at the beginning of Meiji, around 1869, by Izumi Yōsuke, Takayama Kōsuke, and Suzuki Tokujirō, who were inspired by horse-drawn carriages that traveled substantially faster than the palanquin, which was a major means for traveling in Japan until then. The advent of the rickshaw quickly made the palanquin obsolete, and its popularity lasted until the early 1900s, when the horse-drawn carriage, railroad, and electric train were introduced. In 1914, the rickshaw disappeared from the plaza in front of Tokyo station. Rickshaws were also exported to Southeast Asia and Europe. Nihon fūzokushi gakkai, ed., *Nihon fūzokushi jiten* (Kōbundō, 1979), pp. 331–332.

90. Referring to Hanitsu Shrine, where Hoshina Masayuki, the first Aizu daimyo, is enshrined; he was also the younger brother of the third shogun Tokugawa Iemitsu.

91. In Kanagawa prefecture, off Kamakura. Iwamoto-in catered to the shogun and daimyo families during the Tokugawa period.

92. A prominent political figure (1827–77) from Satsuma domain during the closing years of the Tokugawa to early Meiji periods; he was one of the founding members of the Meiji government, although he later clashed with his long-term ally Ōkubo Toshimichi over the government's foreign policy and returned home to Kagoshima.

93. He was born to a *hatamoto* (vassal of the shogun) family in 1823. While serving the Tokugawa *bakufu* as a politician, the liberal-minded Katsu recruited capable people irrespective of their affiliations, even from the Satsuma and Chōshū domains, and endeavored to construct a new nation. Ueda Masaaki and others, eds., *Nihon jinmei jiten* (Sanseidō, 2009), pp.355–356.

94. The Tokugawa period may be subdivided into a number of eras. The Genroku era (1688–1703) was when the country had been fully stabilized and culture flourished, producing a number of enduring works of art and literature.

95. Discussed further in Chapter Three.

96. Koshi is an old term referring to the Hokuriku region (the area facing the Sea of Japan in central Japan).

97. In general, the clans that were Tokugawa allies at the Battle of Sekigahara in 1600 against the Toyotomi, which led the Tokugawa to victory and laid the basis of the Tokugawa hegemony over the country.

98. Hideyoshi (1536/7–98) was Ieyasu's predecessor as a unifier of Japan.

99. A *tozama* daimyo was not a hereditary feudatory of the Tokugawa.

100. Maeda Toshiie (1538–99) was a strong ally of Toyotomi Hideyoshi and after Hideyoshi's death assisted his son Hideyori.

101. The Japanese original reads "*shimo-yashiki*" (lit., lower mansion.) Daimyo, though not all of them, often had more than one residence in Edo: *kami-yashiki* (upper mansion), the main compound where daimyo and his family resided on a regular basis; *shimo-yashiki*, the secondary estate, a kind of a villa often built in the suburbs; and *naka-yashiki* (middle mansion), often used as a substitute for *kami-yashiki*. Further discussion of the daimyo compound is available in Vaporis, *Tour of Duty*, pp. 128–171.

102. He was the *bakufu*'s Senior Councilor during the mid-Tokugawa period.

103. A sweet sponge cake, believed to have been originally introduced by Portuguese. It must have been a highly valued and exotic confectionary at the time.

104. See Chapter Two about inspections of women at *sekisho*.

105. In her diary she mentions that the Naitō clan was related to the Nagoya branch of the Tokugawa. Shiba, *Edoki no onnatachi ga mita Tōkaidō*, p. 220.

106. It is also called "the long bridge of Seta," or "the lying-dragon bridge." The total length is 224 meters, but the bridge is divided into two parts by a small island in the middle of the river: *Ōhashi* (big bridge), 172 m, and *Kobashi* (small bridge), 52 m. In olden times the bridge had a strategically important role in guarding Kyoto. The name of the bridge appears in many works of literature. Tanioka, ed., *Nihon chimei jiten*, p. 681.

107. Legend has it that Murasaki Shikibu, the author of *The Tale of Genji*, retreated to the temple to conceive the basic idea for the tale.

108. She probably saw the *oiran dōchū*, a ritualized procession of a high-ranking courtesan clad in her full formal attire with her attendants and apprentices in a tow, from one place to another within the licensed quarter.

109. James L. McClain and Wakita Osamu, eds., *Osaka: The Merchants' Capital of Early Modern Japan* (Ithaca: Cornell University Press, 1999) provides studies of various aspects of the city.

110. The text is dense with word plays and puns, many of which are untranslatable.

111. Naniwa Harbor. It has been pointed out by Aki Hirota (17, Feb. 2011) that *Naniwazu* also refers to the poem used for children's first calligraphy practice.

112. A melody of *jōruri*. With this pun on *Naniwazu*, according to Hirota, Jūshinin's playful writing can mean "I may not remember how to write properly, but I can sing well."

113. This "eighty-*ri* passing" was also a part of Koganei Yukiko's journey introduced earlier.

Chapter Two

Aspects of Women's Travel

DIFFICULTIES THEY FACED

In the previous chapter, I classified women's travel in the Tokugawa period according to the various motives behind them, and introduced text from some thirty selected travel diaries. In this chapter, we observe certain characteristics of their travel: What difficulties, pleasures or inconveniences did they experience as women? What did they see, hear and learn during their travel?

Sekisho and Inspection of Women

The worst nuisance that accompanied women's travel during the Tokugawa period was inspection at the official *sekisho* checkpoints. In particular, authorities imposed the strictest regulation on two categories: guns brought into, and women leaving Edo, dubbed "in-coming guns and out-going women" (*iri-deppō ni de-onna*). Since the *bakufu* had daimyo families reside in Edo as virtual political hostages, the initial rationale for the regulation was to prevent daimyo wives and children from fleeing back to their domains;[1] though perhaps, the control of women's traffic in general was considered desirable in order to maintain public order and the women's safety.

To clear the *sekisho* inspection, women had to carry a travel permit specifically designed for female travelers. The procedure for issuing the permit was extremely complicated, and the issuers varied depending on the era, as well as the departure location. In the case of Edo, for example, it was the Keeper of Edo Castle who issued permits, while in Kyoto and the western provinces it was the Kyoto Deputy or the Kyoto City Magistrate. When Settsu or Kawachi was the location of departure, the Osaka City Magistrate would issue the permit. There were also cases in which the permit was issued by the daimyo, his chief retainer, or the local magistrate. For commoner women, city magistrates normally provided the permit, but in rural areas the chief priest of a temple or a village headman could sometimes send application to the city magistrate on behalf of a traveler and issue a permit with the magistrate's endorsement.

The required information on a permit included the woman's identity, number of companions, number of vehicles, location of departure, destination, name of applicant, and the name of the issuing office. In particular, the status of the woman had to be clearly distinguished: a Zen nun (the widow or sister of a high-ranking samurai or court noble, who had taken tonsure), a *bikuni* (a disciple nun of a holy priest of Ise Shrine or Zenkō-ji, a lady-in-waiting of the widow of a noble, a nun of Kumano Shrine, etc.), *kamikiri* (those who had their hair cut shorter than normal), *ko-onna* (girls of up to fifteen or sixteen years old, or those wearing kimono with long, trailing sleeves), an insane woman, a prisoner, or a corpse. In addition, the woman had to be described as the mother or daughter of so and so. The stage of any pregnancy and whether the woman's teeth were stained black[2] was among the information to be provided as well. If there were discrepancies between the items mentioned and the actual situation, the permit had to be returned for reapplication. These regulations continued to be observed until 1869, the second year of Meiji.

Crossing barriers without carrying a travel permit was against the law. The code of laws (*Kujigata osadamegaki*) stipulated that the punishment for unpermitted barrier crossing was "crucifixion on the spot," except "a woman who was led by a man to climb the mountain avoiding the barrier is to be deprived of her legal domicile" and "a woman who sneaked through a checkpoint is to be deprived of her legal domicile."

How did women travel under these circumstances? From their travel diaries, we are able to learn or infer how they coped with various challenging situations.

Inspections at Arai

Inoue Tsū-jo, the daughter of Confucian scholar Inoue Motokata of Marugame domain in Sanuki province, headed for Edo in 1681. She was summoned as a tutor for Yōsei-in, the mother of the Marugame daimyo Kyōgoku Takatoyo. On the way, the party was detained at Arai[3] *sekisho* for an item mentioned on her travel permit caught the attention of an official; the twenty-two-year-old Tsū-jo had identified herself as *onna* (woman) in her papers, naturally, whereas a female traveler wearing a kimono with long, trailing sleeves, like herself, was supposed to be defined as *ko-onna* (girl, young woman). To have her permit replaced with a correct description, she had to send a messenger back to Osaka, and the procedure forced the party stay at an Arai inn for as long as six days.

> It saddened me a great deal to have to go through all this trouble. Why on earth had I not known this in advance and prepared appropriately? I felt frustrated at myself.

> In traveling clothes—
> unable to pass the barrier
> of Arai ("the rough waters"),
> I am overcome by melancholy,
> my sleeves wet[4] by rough waves

Tsū-jo lamented in her diary "*Tōkai kikō*" (Travel along the Eastern Sea) over the inconveniences of travel, writing, "There are many discomforts a woman must endure." As a matter of fact, she had had to stay in Osaka for two days to have her original travel permit issued by the City Magistrate, but now her messenger was required to return to Osaka to obtain a revised pass for her. She submitted the new travel permit to Arai *sekisho*, and the party was at last allowed to pass. From the ferry at the *sekisho* they sailed across the lake to Maisaka.

Tsuchiya Ayako[5] crossed the lake from Maisaka to Arai when heading for Sakai. She described her experience undergoing inspection in her diary "*Tabi no inochige*" (A Journey with a Writing Brush):

> The ferry arrived on the other side of the lake at noon. I received inspection after transferring from the boat to a palanquin. A woman in her fifties wearing something on her head came around, and began the procedure. She appeared countrified, but her manners were polite in an old-fashioned way. The officials busily exchanged words in loud voices. We spent the night at an inn in Hashimoto. There had been a bridge over the lake in olden times. Hearing the story of how it had decayed over the years made me feel somewhat nostalgic. Now, it became a place for the traveler to be inspected, as at Hakone *sekisho*. With these strict inspections, we women cannot easily reverse our route to go home no matter how homesick we feel. It made me sad and lonely.

> Having traveled
> far away from home in Ōmi,
> have I reached
> the shore, where the ancient
> bridge is no more

It was almost one thousand years prior, in 884, during the reign of Emperor Yōzei, when the Hamana Bridge was built over the lake in Tōtōmi province.

The bridge had long decayed and disappeared, and now a ferry boat was the only means across the lake.

Inspections at Hakone

There were fifty-three *sekisho* established during the Edo period, and Hakone was known as one of the four major barriers, along with Arai on the Tōkaidō, and Usui and Kiso-Fukushima on the Nakasendō. The inspection of women at Hakone was especially strict, as described by Inoue Tsū-jo in another diary, "*Kika nikki*" (A Homeward Journey).

Tsū-jo, who waited on Yōsei-in at the daimyo's Edo mansion,[6] instructed the women of the family in the literary arts. Earning her mistress's firm confidence, she often exchanged *waka* and *kanshi* with dignitaries at Yōsei-in's salon, who would praise Tsū-jo's talents as "equal to those of Murasaki Shikibu and Sei Shōnagon of the Heian Period." She spent nine fruitful years there, and when Yōsei-in died in 1689, Tsū-jo resigned the position and left for Marugame the same year, and was missed greatly by the people of the Edo mansion.

Her return trip was easier, accompanied by her younger brother Masumoto. She enjoyed the scenery from inside her palanquin, feeling "thoroughly protected and relaxed." Still, the thought of the *sekisho* at Hakone and Arai concerned her. Masumoto had the necessary travel permits issued by the Keeper of Edo Castle for those barriers before the party left Edo; nonetheless, the inspection of women at Hakone was strict.

We arrived at the *sekisho*. I waited in my palanquin, while my brother submitted the travel permit and asked for further instructions from the officials. Then he called me over, and I had my palanquin moved towards the guard. Masumoto told me that they had an old woman summoned to inspect both my female attendant and myself. The woman inspector did a body check on me, combing through my hair, as well. She was a coarse and uncultured woman, and though old, quite healthy and strong. She sat closely by my side and questioned me in a throaty voice. I was frightened and nervous, wondering what would happen next. Then the officials asked her various questions in detail to receive information about me. They told my brother that everything fit the description and that we were allowed to go through. While I had been sure that there had been no error on the travel permit, I still felt my heart racing once exposed to such a forbidding atmosphere. When the inspection ended, therefore, I was extremely pleased and immediately had the attendants gather to leave the site together. I had my hair fixed when the party reached the top of the hill.

The strict inspection of papers by the guards and body check by a female inspector must have substantially diminished the joy of women's travel.

Evading Barriers

Inspection of women travelers apparently eased towards the end of the Tokugawa period. When the actual conditions of an individual did not match the description on her travel permit, it seems that officials at times had the woman change her clothes or hairstyle to erase the discrepancies and let her pass. In fact, we rarely find travel diaries of later years that complain of the unpleasantness and inconveniences that Inoue Tsū-jo experienced. What draw our attention instead are the records of women travelers without travel permits who would avoid inspections by taking byroads around the *sekisho*.

Oda Ieko, fifty-three-year-old wife of a merchant of Onga in Chikuzen province, traveled with three women friends and three male attendants in 1841. On their five-month journey from the first month to the sixth month, they travelled approximately 3200 kilometers. They sailed across the Seto Inland Sea, visited Osaka, Nara, Yoshino, and on 3.9 visited Ise Shrine. Then Ieko and her companions decided to extend their journey to Zenkō-ji, a route for which they did not have travel permits. "We arrived in Tsumagome. At the foot of the bridge we entered a back road that bypassed the Fukushima *bansho*.[7] Women often take this route. The road was deep in the mountains and quite steep. Climbing the pass was so hard on us." Obviously Ieko's party, without an appropriate pass, chose to climb the steep slopes to avoid Kiso-Fukushima *sekisho*, where the inspection of women was notoriously strict.

On 3.27, after offering prayers at Zenkō-ji, they headed for Nikkō. There was Usui *sekisho* in Kōzuke province, the strictest barrier on the Nakasendō. Her diary "*Azumaji nikki*" (A Journey to the East) describes how they managed to evade it: "To avoid Usui *sekisho*, we left Oiwake in Shinano province heading southeast, traveled 16 kilometers, and arrived in the town of Hatsutoya. From there we climbed steep hills, grabbing the ivy and vines, and hanging on to roots and rocks. We barely made it to the pass."

Similar experiences are described in other diaries. Miyake Yoshiemon and his wife Yae of Fuwa in Mino province faced difficulties at various barriers when they traveled to Zenkō-ji in 1863.7. They recorded their experience in their journal "*Zenkō-ji tateyama sankei tabinikki*" (A Pilgrimage to Zenkō-ji and Tateyama): "There was a *bansho* of the Sakakibara clan in a region called Sekigawa, where women were not allowed to pass. We therefore asked the inn master for a guide, who led us to climb underneath the fence of the *bansho* to pass through."

The barrier mentioned above is the one at Sekigawa along the Mikunikaidō in Kubiki, Echigo province. It was under the control of the Sakakibaras, the Takada daimyo. Yae and her husband hired a guide, who led them to crawl through a "doggy gate" (*inukuguri*) in the fence at night[8] to bypass the *sekisho*. It was an unpermitted barrier crossing, and therefore a felony. But the officials seem to have turned a blind eye to those illegal acts.

Guide Fee for Evading Barriers

Bypassing barriers or taking "women's road" byroads to avoid checkpoints was of course dangerous and risky, and naturally it cost a certain amount of money to hire a guide for the endeavor.

Yae and her husband paid sixty *mon* to the guide to avoid Ichiburi *sekisho* controlled by the Sakakibaras. When they reached Yanagase of Ika in Ōmi province, they had been unaware of the existence of a *sekisho* and were unprepared for inspection, triggering the guards' severe scolding. No matter how they pleaded, the answers were "No, no!" Being at a loss, the couple returned to the inn and asked its owner to be an intermediary; through him they donated to the guards fifty *mon* as "small gift-money for snacks." With this donation they were allowed to pass the *sekisho*.

> Thank God—
> money can open the impossible gate
> that would otherwise be tightly shut,
> Does the gate keeper have
> such a corruptible heart, indeed?

There are other diaries that record payments of fees to guides for the purpose of avoiding barriers. In 1862.4, Toyo, the mother of merchant Ōsakaya Haruemon of Yamagata, left for a two-and-a-half-month journey to Zenkō-ji, Edo and Kamakura, probably to celebrate her sixtieth birthday. Her "*Zenkō-ji dōchū nikki*" (A Journey via Zenkō-ji) shows that her party paid the guide thirty-six *mon* per person for bypassing Sekigawa *sekisho* and one hundred *mon* at Hachizaki *sekisho* in Takada domain.

Imano Ito, a merchant's wife of Honjō in Dewa province, went on a pilgrimage to Ise Shrine with the wife of Satō Nagaemon and two male attendants in 1862. In her "*Sangū dōchū shoyōki*" (Cash Book for the Pilgrimage to Ise) here and there we find payments of guide fees for evading *sekisho*: forty *mon* for "guiding through the women's road" bypassing Sekigawa *sekisho*, thirty-six *mon* for "guiding through Sekigawa at night" on her way back from Zenkō-ji, sixty *mon* for "guiding at night" at Ichiburi *sekisho*, and twenty-five *mon* at Daishō-ji *sekisho* (in present-day Ishikawa prefecture). At Hakone she paid one hundred *mon* for "guidance around the *sekisho*," an amount considerably higher than at the other places. In the preface of her diary, Ito states that she decided to travel on the spur of the moment and left without telling other people. She was probably therefore without a travel permit, and her party often hired guides to travel along women's routes and hidden paths. At times she had travel permits issued on her way at fees varying from fifteen to twenty-eight *mon*. Ito had her hair done frequently during her journey, and considering it cost about thirty *mon*, the guide fee for bypassing *sekisho* and obtaining travel permits on the way were apparently not outrageously expensive.

Going through the application procedure for travel permits and receiving strict inspections at *sekisho* were inconvenient and often unpleasant experiences, which women would have desired to avoid if at all possible. Sometimes they simply did not have the time to obtain a permit, as in Ito's case. Obviously, money sometimes provided a shortcut around these obstacles.

Off-Limit Areas for Women

There were many shrines and holy mountains that forbade women's entrance, posting notices that women were not allowed. Among those were the famous Mt. Kōya and Mt. Ōmine, where women were allowed only in designated areas or buildings. The tradition is believed to have started based on religious laws that perceived women as unclean due to their menstruation and childbirth,[9] or as an undesirable temptation for Buddhist monks strictly observing abstinence during training. In addition the decline of women's social and economic status in pre- to early modern Japan perhaps contributed to the erection of the "women not allowed" boards at various sites. It might also be said that such restrictions were for the protection of women, preventing them from entering dangerous areas. In either case such notice boards were a nuisance for women travelers who wished to visit the holy sites and mountains.

"I rested for a while in front of Mishima-myōjin Shrine. But as a woman, with the possibility of defilement, I was not able to offer prayers in the shrine," wrote *shirabyōshi* entertainer[10] Take-jo in her travel diary "*Kōshi michi no ki*" (Kōshi Travel Diary), who was praised for her literary talent by National studies scholars such as Murata Harumi and Shimizu Hamaomi.

Yamanashi Shigako, in her "*Haru no michikusa*" (Dawdling along Spring Roads) wrote about Mt. Shosha, when she traveled to the western regions with her son: "This is a holy mountain which prohibits women from entering. I went as far as the women's hall (*nyonindō*), while the rest of the party climbed to the top of the mountain. . . . They went to the monk's residential quarters. At the women's hall I met a woman from Higo province. I talked with her all night long."

Kurosawa Toki was also stopped at the women's hall, she writes in her "*Jōkyō nikki*" (Journey to Kyoto), when she visited Mt. Togakushi on her way to Edo: "I could not go further inside the premises to enter the other hall, where no women were allowed. Near the rock called *bikuni ishi* (the nun's rock) was the *nyonindō*." Legend had it that a woman had been changed into the rock now called *bikuni ishi* when she had attempted to go beyond the boundary. There was a sign on Koshimizugahara that marked the boundary line for women, according to the study *Togakushimura ni okeru kinsekibun* (Epigraphs in Togakushi Village). On the stone monument erected in 1795 was carved "The middle and main halls on your right both prohibit women's entrance" and "Women's route is to the middle hall on your left."

River Ferries

Between Shimada in Suruga province and Kanaya in Tōtōmi province was the ferry across the Ōi River, a notoriously challenging area along the Tōkaidō, as described in song, "Even on horseback a traveler can manage to pass the steep mountain of Hakone but how on earth could he pass across the frightening waters of the Ōi River?"

The *haikai* poetess Shokyū-ni of Okazaki in Kyoto left for a pilgrimage through Ōshū in 1771, following the route that Bashō had traveled decades before. For the fifty-eight-year-old nun, the ferry across the Ōi River was an experience she could not endure without murmuring sutras, as she described in her "*Akikaze no ki*" (Autumn Winds Diary):

> Soon after passing Kikukawa I arrived at the Ōi River. The ferry had been halted until yesterday due to the high water level caused by the recent heavy rain. Luckily, they resumed service today. I was very glad. When my turn came, I was hoisted up on an interestingly arranged board. Several porters carried the board along, while the tall waves washed their shoulders. I was frightened to death and was chanting sutras with my eyes tightly shut until reaching the other shore.

The post stations near the river would be swollen with travelers, including daimyo alternate-attendance processions, when the ferry services were closed. Often, travelers were stopped for more than ten days during the rainy season, which would upset their itineraries and cost them extra money for the prolonged stay. They were indeed at a loss for what to do when faced with "the frightening waters of the Ōi River." What Shokyū-ni describes as "an interestingly arranged board" above refers to a kind of a litter called a *rendai*, whose structure varied depending on the fees charged: some without handrails, some with handrails on one side, and others on all four sides. Daimyo typically used the ones with handrails on all four sides. In addition to *rendai* was the piggyback ferry, both conducted by ferry porters. The river's normal level of water was said to be about 75 centimeters deep; crossing on horseback was stopped when the water reached the level of 105 centimeters and crossing on foot at 135 centimeters. Travelers were often terrified in the shallows, too, where the porters would carry them while running as fast as flying birds. Following are the impressions of the river recorded in Tsuchiya Ayako's diary "*Tabi no inochige*" (A Journey with a Writing Brush):

> I crossed the Ōi River around two o'clock in the afternoon. It was indeed the largest river on the Tōkaidō as I had been told, an intimidating site. The water level had decreased recently. On the vast shallows were scary, coarse looking men, half naked, gathering around me. They quickly roped my palanquin, held it above their shoulders, shouted "Yo-ho!" and sped across the dry riverbed like flying birds. It felt as if I was half dreaming, with my head and feet swinging around, feeling dizzy and having difficulty breathing. I was worried about how my children were coping with this but could do nothing. . . . Presently they ran ashore, then rotated my palanquin and quickly lowered it. I felt as if I had been pushed back to fall into a ravine thousands of meters deep. When the river crossing had been completed, the women were all so pale that the people around us laughed loudly.

Seasickness and Waiting for Winds

During sea voyages, too, travelers often had to stay in port for days, waiting for favorable winds. Fujiki Ichi's party had to wait ten days for the wind at the port of Murozumi when the bridal procession sailed the Seto Inland Sea, as has been mentioned earlier. After finally leaving the port, however, everyone then became seasick due to the high waves on the winter sea, and lay down in the bottom of the ship, unable to appreciate the picturesque scenery.

Kōsei-in, the widow of the Sadowara daimyo Shimazu Hisataka, obtained permission to go home to her parents' house in Kagoshima six years after the death of her husband. At the beginning of the ninth month of 1669, Kōsei-in left Edo, traveled along the Tōkaidō, visited the Kyoto area, and from Osaka sailed the Seto Inland Sea to the west. Her diary "*Azuma no yume*" (Dreams of the East) describes some of the hardships she endured during the journey.

> We departed under moonlight on the twentieth and sailed along the Sea of Iyo. In the strong winds and high waves the boat pitched high and low. I became seasick and felt terrible, but of course could not command it to stop. Arriving at last at Saganoseki in Bungo province, I was too seasick to travel any further and borrowed a room at a fisherman's hut to lie down. My ladies-in-waiting also lay down around me, talking to each other how terrified they had been during the voyage. I really felt the same.

Hidaka Tsutako's diary records a similar anecdote: Their boat encountered rough waves when they had just passed Matsuyama of Iyo province, when a woman, terribly seasick, cried out, imploring "Oh what will become of us! Please, any port will do, bring the boat to a stop, please!" Seasickness was indeed one of the hardships that greatly troubled travelling women.

Illness and Death away from Home

When commoners traveled, they were required to carry the identification document known as *ōrai tegata*, which was different from the *sekisho tegata* that the ruling class carried. On the paper were recorded the name and address of the carrier, and additional information was required of a female traveler about her family relationships (mother of such-and-such, daughter of so-and-so). The document also included a paragraph requesting accommodation in the event that the traveler could not reach her destination before the sun set, and for burial in case of death, following the custom of the region. In some cases, there would be a note that there was no need to inform her home of the traveler's death.

Shokyū-ni, mentioned earlier, fell ill during her journey in Ōshū and stayed in bed for forty days. She felt helpless and terribly homesick, suffering from a grave illness and nearly losing her life. Fortunately she survived, thanks to the doctor and her acquaintances, who treated and nursed her warmly. She wrote in her diary "*Akikaze no ki*" (Autumn Winds Diary):

> My condition gets worse day by day, and I can hardly carry out daily activities. Being over a thousand kilometers away from home, I grieve over my old body that may not be able to survive. . . . I asked where the wind was blowing from. They said it was from the west. I felt deeply homesick and kept on looking at the moon until it declined.

Okada Itsu also experienced an unexpected sojourn at Fukushima in Mutsu province due to her companion's illness on her return to Kyoto after resigning from her official duties at Matsumae. She called a doctor for her and nursed her day and night for a week, but felt entirely lost, writing, "No change in her condition, and I am at a loss what to do. All I can do is to lament over the melancholy of travel."

Onoike Matsuko of Hayashima in Bizen province had a daughter and a son, but her husband left the family, having lost his fortune after being tricked by an acquaintance. Matsuko managed the household and raised the children, and when they grew up, she took to the road for a pilgrimage across the country. She visited the Western circuit of thirty-three Kannon temples and extended her journey to Ezo (present-day Hokkaidō), where she sojourned for about one year before returning home. When she reached Ōdate in Dewa province, Matsuko fell ill. In spite of the inn master's warm nursing, she died in 1809.11, in her fifties. Although travelers who died during their journeys were normally buried where they passed, with no particular notice sent home, Matsuko's death was reported to her family through the good will of the Satakes, the local daimyo family. Matsuko's son Ihei made the long journey to Ōdate, expressed the family's profound gratitude to the inn master and other people, and returned home with his mother's remains, a lock of hair, her travel diary and *waka* poems she had composed. Unfortunately neither the travel diary nor poems have been preserved, nor is it known why Matsuko travelled to Ezo. Only one of the *waka* she wrote is found in *Ruidai kibikoku kashū* (A collection of *waka* from Kibi province classified according to themes) edited by Matsuda Yamadakyū in 1848:

> I composed this poem at Ezo in autumn, 1807.
>
> > Like the blue of the ocean—
> > is my mind, so clear, unclouded with
> > any shade of worry,
> > so, too, is the moon of the autumn night
> > shining above the Chishima islands in Ezo

Having raised her children, with the son inheriting his father's name and her daughter married into another family, Matsuko must have been deeply content when she looked up at the moon in the clear autumn sky. Nothing else of her own writing is available now, leaving us no clue as to what she had to say about her life. But with this *waka* we know that Matsuko had accomplished an ambitious, extensive journey before departing this world, a journey on a scale that many women at the time might have found inconceivable.

JOYS OF TRAVEL

Experiencing the Wider World

Travel was full of challenges and difficulties for women of the early modern era, but it provided great joy, as well. Once on the road they could actually experience that which they had heard and read about. It was more than just visiting temples and shrines or places of scenic beauty and historic interest. They would climb mountains, cross the ridges and plains, ride horses, travel in palanquins, stroll through the fields, collect sea shells on the beach, get on boats, sail across the inland sea by steamship, lodge at an inn, drink tea at a tea stall or go shopping. Each was a valuable, fresh experience, rarely a part of people's daily lives at home.

The seasonal flora and fauna must have appeared much more vivid than in books. Appreciating nature deeply through all their five senses, women travelers composed deeply-felt poems.

> Evening cicadas
> with your loud chorus—
> Are you trying to make me forget
> the loneliness of traveling through fields of
> grass wet with dew?

> Whose robe is this
> left on a tree branch, I asked,
> to which replied
> the cicadas in their vigorous chorus
> "it's mine," "it's mine," "it's mine."

The above poems are both from "*Ikaho-ki*" (Ikaho Diary) by Nakagawa Man, the wife of the Oka daimyo in Bungo province. In 1639, when the rulers were in turmoil due to the Shimabara Rebellion,[11] Man set out on a journey to see the beautiful mountain villages in Ikaho and the various flowers found in the Musashino grove. Passing through Musashino on her way, she was greatly comforted by the singing of the evening cicadas and was inspired to compose those verses; both sound as if she was conversing directly with the insects, a theme she might not have conceived had she been sitting in her living room.

Chiyo-jo, the *haikai* poetess of Mattō in Kaga province, who traveled to various places in the Kantō and Kansai regions, did not leave much of a diary, but her works of *haikai* reveal to us her footsteps. When she was sixty years old in 1762, she attended the memorial service for Rennyo[12] at Yoshizaki-gobō.[13]

I went to visit Yoshizaki. Deeply grateful and moved by its ambience, I offered prayers and composed this:

> With my head bowed
> did I see the gentle petals of violets,
> the seat of Buddha

Surrounded by the beauty of nature, Chiyo-jo was obviously jubilant and able to experience Buddha's great mercy.

Escaping from Daily Routine

Travel in those times absolutely required physical fitness and vitality. It made women face various situations that often forced them to make their own judgments and decisions. Once on the road, they could not afford to merely remain obedient wives or daughters, as moral texts for women instructed. In fact, normal precepts for women would be of no particular help in managing the dynamic relationships with their travel companions throughout their long journeys. They also had to weather winds, rains, and thunderstorms, endure the hardships of climbing mountains, crossing rivers and ridges, and many more. Travel required a new resourcefulness of them.

Enthusiastically touring various places, women enjoyed the experience of spending time and money for themselves. They found the time to live for and reflect upon themselves, perhaps leading to new discoveries about themselves, as well.

At times, there were women who traveled disguised as nuns or clad like men, perhaps to avoid various nuisances that might bedevil female travelers. In her disguised identity she could escape her routine lifestyle, an opportunity to learn about various aspects of the world that she might not have noticed otherwise.

Tsuchiya Ayako was quite impressed by the richness of the land of Fuchū in Suruga province, the place where Tokugawa Ieyasu lived his last years after handing over his position to Hidetada, the second shogun, though still remaining a powerful political figure. Ayako could not help but contemplate the differences between the lively farmers of Fuchū and their poor counterparts working the impoverished land in the mountains of Hakone whom she had witnessed the previous day:

> There are those who live on spacious lands, and those in cramped areas. There are those who are happy, and those who are not. Heaven must have determined the destiny of each human being. Are we not endowed with the power to change our destiny as we wish? Perhaps, we ought to leave everything to the reasons of Heaven. Perhaps we are not to lament over our fate.

Ayako was said to be "unusually educated for a woman and competitive, strong-minded," "not in a loving relationship with her husband," and an "erudite lady who keeps her husband under her thumb," which were not considered positive womanly attributes at the time. She was well versed in *kanshi*, too, and had a tendency to find the reason and logic of things. A woman of this nature might not have been too appealing to men in general in that milieu. The above quote from her diary seems to imply her own constrained feelings as a woman, as if she is convincing herself not to lament over her lot.

Expanding Circles of Friends

Travel brought women opportunities for socializing with people. Women were, in fact, amazingly active in making the acquaintance of people of taste in various places. A visit to a friend would attract like-minded people in the area, who would gather to compose poems together, and then might introduce the traveler to other people of taste at the next planned stop.

Some kept records of the people whom they met during their journeys: their names, pen names, villages, towns, provinces, and so forth.

Hara Saihin, introduced in the previous chapter, kept a record entitled *"Kinranbo"* (Helleborine Orchid Notes), which carries one hundred thirty entries, many of whom were Confucian scholars and their close associates, including Matsuzaki Kōdō of Kakegawa domain, Koga Kokudō, his brother Dōan, both of Saga domain, and many others. At the beginning of *"Kinranbo"* is written "the eleventh year of the Bunsei era," indicating that Saihin made friends with those people when she traveled to Kyoto and Edo at the age of thirty-one in 1828. The number of her friends must have multiplied during her twenty-year stay in Edo, also including her tours of the Bōsō Peninsula, and her travel throughout Kyūshū when she was about sixty years old.

A *waka* poetess and an enigmatic figure, Nakayama Miya, who was born in Kyoto towards the end of the Tokugawa period and often traveled to the western regions clad as a nun, also kept a record of acquaintances entitled *"Jinmei-oboe"* (Address Book). Those listed in it are renowned scholars, Shinto priests, Buddhist priests, wealthy merchants and clansmen of the western provinces, most of whom were poets of *waka* or *kanshi* as well as leaders of the loyalist movement of the time. Perhaps Miya traveled on a mission to collect intelligence and provide it to certain people. On the list are found the names of loyalists, including the *waka* poet Takahashi Masakaze and Ōkubo Ichizō (later Toshimichi)[14] of Satsuma, Yamagata Shōsuke (later Aritomo)[15] and Katori Motohiko of Chōshū, and Fukuba Bisei of Tsuwano. The number of the names on the list amounts to over four hundred in total.

Female travelers also became acquainted with various other people during their journeys: those who happened to stay in the same inns, local residents who showed them kindness, and other travelers whom they encountered on the road.

Learning Both Artistic and Practical Matters

We have observed in the previous chapter that Kikusha-ni of Nagato spent over half of her seventy-four years learning from various masters the arts of *haikai*, *waka*, *kanshi*, drawing and painting, tea ceremony and *koto*-playing.

Like Kikusha-ni, many people traveled for training. They learned from nature. They trained in the arts through associating with the masters and friends whom they sought and met at various places. Especially in the world of *haikai*, it was critical for the poet to participate in the communal composition of a sequence of verses with like-minded people, a highly intellectual activity through which the participants create a microcosm of the poetic art. It required strong focus to work with others as one creative mind; a form of poetic training that *haikai* poets sought to experience through travel, away from the environments to which they were accustomed.

Igarashi Hamamo, the daughter of the village headman of Machida in Musashi province, traveled with her father Umeo to the western regions in 1806, when she was thirty-three years old.[16] They participated in some one hundred *haikai* gatherings, creating sequences of verses in various provinces, such as Nagasaki, Kokura in Chikuzen, Yamaga, Shōbara in Bingo, Kasaoka in Bitchū, Shōdoshima in Sanuki, Hiramatsu in Ōmi, and Owari. Among those were eighteen groups limited to women only, whose compositions she published as a collection entitled "*Yaeyamabuki*" (Double-Petaled Japanese Roses) in 1810.

It was not only the art of literature that women learned through travel. They acquired a sense of distance by walking, learned the prices of commodities by purchasing various items and paying for accommodations and transportation, and a sense of economy in general through money exchange. They also learned how the transportation systems actually functioned by purchasing travel permits and paying guide fees for the bypassing of barriers.

Deepened Conjugal Love

Married couples, too, traveled and composed journals; some wrote together and others independently. The Confucian scholar Kaibara Ekken and his wife Tōken, of Fukuoka in Chikuzen province, journeyed to various regions of the country. They left a large number of travel accounts, to which Tōken's contribution is believed to have been substantial.

Takebe Ayatari,[17] the versatile intellectual known as a *haikai* poet, scholar of National studies, author of popular literature, and artist, was the son of the councilor of Tsugaru domain. He ran away from home when he was twenty, as a result of having committed adultery with his sister-in-law. He lived the rest of his life as a wandering writer-artist. In his last years Ayatari took his wife Kitsu along on his travels, who assisted him as his personal secretary; she kept contacts with his disciples across the country and took notes of his travel accounts and essays. Among those travel accounts are "*Ume nikki*" (Plum Blossom Diary) describing their travel to Yamato and Uji, "*Sakura nikki*" (Cherry Blossom Diary) on the journey to Yoshino, "*Unohana nikki*" (Deutzia Blossom Diary) on the pilgrimage to Ise, and "*Higashi no michiyukiburi*" (Journey to the Eastern Provinces) about their final journey to Kyoto, Shinano, Kōzuke, and Edo in 1773. In this last work are included the memoirs of Ayatari's final days and verses of *waka* commemorating the first anniversary of his death, all written by Kitsu. The diary shows the couple's strong bond and deep love.

> Looking up at the sky
> prostrating myself on the ground,
> I pray for his return—
> Could I not stop you, my love,
> who left for the journey to heaven

Kitsu was devastated at Ayatari's death. All she could do to console her heart was to remember the last several years, when the two were never apart from each other.

Morioka Fuboku and his wife Fuyū, who ran a shipping agency in a village on the Noto Peninsula, were both *haikai* poets. They left home for a journey of *haikai* composition in 1776, with a travel sack and walking sticks. The couple visited the grave of Bashō at Gichū-ji in Ōtsu, toured historical spots in Kyoto, and appreciated the eight views at Ōmi (*Ōmi-hakkei*). Then they headed for Fukui via the Hokkokudō. They often composed *hokku* to each other on a theme. The following are included in their "*Haikai sode miyage*" (Souvenir of Haikai Tour):

> At Karasaki[18]
> In Karasaki—
> cicadas sing in the daylight, like
> the sound of drizzling rain
>
> —Fuboku

> Above the pine tree
> gently hangs the clear moon
> radiating cool
>
> —Fuyū

Arakida Rei, the foremost author of historical tales during the Tokugawa period, was the adopted daughter of her uncle, a priest of the Ise Shrine; her husband Ietada married into that family. Ietada understood Rei's talent well and supported her creative activities. The couple, though not well-off, often traveled together to further Rei's learning, by visiting places of scenic beauty and historic interest as well as calling on intellectuals in various regions of the country.

In 1777, when Rei-jo[19] was forty six, they traveled to Kyoto, Yoshino, and Nara, which culminated in her work "*Hatsuuma no nikki*" (First Horse Day Diary).[20] After another voyage together to Yamato, Kyoto, and Harima in 1782, when she was fifty-two, Rei-jo wrote a diary entitled "*Nochinouma no nikki*" (Later Horse Day Diary). To save money, the couple traveled without attendants, carrying their luggage all by themselves. In her front travel sack hanging from her neck were a comb, a mirror, sheets of rice paper, thread, needles, incense, etc., and on her back she carried rain gear. Afraid of being embarrassed by the frugality of their travel, they did not even tell their folk their expected date of return, and came home after dark to avoid people's eyes. Nonetheless, their journeys were rich in spirit; their goal was to visit as many locations as possible to compose poems and meet as many intellectuals as they could. In her travel diaries we witness Ietada's sincere devotion to his wife and her creative activities. When she hurt her leg, he would carry her on his back as they continued their journey, as recorded in their "*Nanto Kyoto Osaka junrei dōchū ikken nikki*" (Journey to Nara, Kyoto, and Osaka). In traveling they must have confirmed their deep affection for one another, to a degree that they might not have experienced in their ordinary life at home.

WHAT THEY OBSERVED AND ACQUIRED

Places of Scenic Beauty and Historic Interest

Once on the road, people tried to maximize the number of sites to visit within their limited itineraries. Travelers at the time normally left their lodgings before dawn and tried to reach the next stop during daylight; at times, however, they would walk until darkness fell, especially in the case of private travel. People did not want to miss any places of historic interest or scenic beauty on their way; even during a sea voyage, they would often have the boat anchored in port for additional tours on shore. When that was not possible, they made sure to verbally express their thoughts on those places. For poets of *waka* and *haikai*, one major purpose of their journeys was to compose their own original verses at famous places depicted in ancient poems or relevant to literary history.

Nakamura Ito, the wife of an Edo purveyor of *tatami* (straw matting)[21] to the *bakufu*, went on a pilgrimage to Ise Shrine with several people in 1825. They traveled the Tōkaidō on their way to Ise, visited Yoshino, Nara, Suma, Akashi, Miyajima, Konpira Shrine, and came home via the Kisoji road. With a relatively leisurely pace of about twenty kilometers a day during the eighty-day journey, Ito was deeply content to have visited well over one hundred places,[22] according to her "*Ise mōde no nikki*" (Diary of an Ise Pilgrimage).

Local Specialties

Women travelers enjoyed sampling and purchasing various local specialties. Let us observe some of the items described in their travel diaries.

Along the Tōkaidō, first there were abalones and seashell wares in Fujisawa, and chestnut powder cakes between Yoshiwara and Kambara. Jūshin-in, disappointed at the chestnut-powder cakes, wrote, "I was curious what it would be like, but it was just a pathetic rice cake with chestnut powder sprinkled on it." She, however, bought agate works there, and plenty of sea bream at Okitsu, the famous specialty of the place. There were also *oke-sushi* (pail sushi) in Koyoshida, rice cakes covered with soybean powder in Abekawa, and rice-cake candies (thin rice cakes with glutinous malt-sugar inside) in Sayono-Nakayama that were said to be good for the health of the aged. The town Ōhama next to Okazaki was famous for *soba* (buckwheat noodles). Jūshin-in bought metalwork at Chiriu, and the tie-dyed cotton of Arimatsu, renowned as the best merchandise along the Tōkaidō. Grilled clams in Kuwana were famous but were apparently not so tasty, as was often the case with local specialties. According to Jūshin-in, "It was not good, though I had been told otherwise." But she was satisfied with *sekinoto mochi*, the rice cake named after the renowned temple Seki-no-jizō at the Suzuka *sekisho*. She wrote, "While resting I ate *sekinoto mochi*. It was the tastiest delicacy I have had so far along the highway." Her verdict, however, seems to have been biased by her extreme hunger at the time.[23] At Minakuchi, there was handiwork such as wicker baskets, pot stands and hats. Tsuchiyama was famous for a confectionary called *akebono*. Kusatsu was well-known for gourds and the rice cake called *ubagamochi*. This cake pleased Nakamura Ito, who wrote, "Kusatsu's specialty *ubagamochi* tastes excellent, and people are crazy about it," even composing a humorous verse, "*Ubagamochi* / of Kusatsu that appears / to be *kusa* (=stinky, punning on Kusatsu) / surprises you once eaten / with its superb taste." Jūshin-in, on the other hand, was obviously not impressed, "I ate *ubagamochi*, which people praise so much. But the cake was so soggy that I found it almost inedible." In Osaka there were the famous steamed buns of a long-established shop named Toraya.

There were other places that also produced noodles, sushi, handcrafts, ceramics, straw mats, etc. as their local specialties. Jūshin-in bought plenty of straw mats in Bingo province, called *Bingo goza*, though they were of inferior quality, since "those of good quality had been all shipped to Edo and were out of stock." She was also quite interested in the rocks of Iyo province during her sea voyage. She boarded a small boat, had it rowed to the beach, and collected a variety of rocks herself. "I placed the rocks on the plank to observe them well. I was pleased to find that each one of them had a unique shape."

What drew women's attention most among local specialties were over-whelmingly food items, which could be consumed on the spot. It would be too burdensome to purchase inedible souvenirs to carry around during their journeys, unless they were women of daimyo families accompanied by a number of attendants and porters.

Encounters with Other Lifestyles

While traveling, women encountered people of various stations and plights, and expressed warm interest and compassion toward them.

Oda Ieko, the wife of a wealthy merchant of Chikuzen province, described in "*Azumaji nikki*" (A Journey to the East) the villagers she saw in a village in the Kisoji Pass on their way to Zenkō-ji in 1841:

> There were several houses along the pass, with the Kiso River flowing on the left. A few women came out of a house by the road. One's hair was so unkempt and clothes so shabby that I could hardly tell whether it was a man or a woman. Another was wearing an old, worn out garment with an awkwardly large family crest dyed on it. The size of the kimono did not fit her and her bare shoulders were showing. I was told that she made her living by selling handmade combs. . . . Among them was a woman in her forties. As I sat down to rest, the woman took out a comb and asked me to buy it. I asked the price, which was very low. She told us that since their family didn't have any land to work, the women made those combs for their living. We were all so moved to witness such poverty, and everyone bought a couple of combs from her.

Their poverty was perhaps caused by the recent great famine. Ieko could not help but reflect upon her privileged life that allowed her to enjoy travel, and was deeply moved by the plight of the poor women. Ieko's heart also ached when she heard from a villager that they had barely survived on small shoots of bamboo for a couple of years during the famine.

In the fourth month of 1868, Matsudaira Jitei-in Takeko, the wife of the Kawagoe daimyo in Musashi province, went home to Saga. The ostensible reason for her homecoming was recuperation at a local hot spring resort, arranged by her father, the Saga daimyo. In fact, her father Nabeshima Nao-masa was concerned about his daughter's safety should anything have hap-pened in Edo during that tumultuous year. On her way, she stopped over at Kyoto, where her father was also staying at the time. He warmly entertained her during her sojourn at the capital. One day he accompanied her to the temple Byōdō-in at Uji. On their return home, she saw tea-picking at a tea plantation; she was quite fascinated, as she depicted the scene in her diary "*Matsu no shizuku*" (Dew Drops on Pine Trees):

Humble women were picking tea, clad in neat outfits, their hair adorned with pretty ornaments. Under their sashes were uniformly tucked the so-called tea-picking towels. They sang together while picking the leaves. Their chorus was never out of tune and the entire scene was so pleasant and refreshing. The view was even superior to those rendered in paintings.

Zuishin-in Yoriko, the wife of the Sadowara daimyo, also paid close attention to the livelihoods of commoners. In March, 1863, while passing Yamaga in Higo province on her way from Edo to Sadowara, she saw farmers planting rice seedlings in a drizzling rain. She expressed her gratitude towards the farmers with a verse of *waka* in her diary:[24]

After we left Yamaga, it started raining, preventing us from making much progress on the road. Yet we managed to visit the temple of the late lord Katō Kiyomasa. The road continued to be challenging, but the rain changed to a drizzle around noon. I composed a verse when I saw peasants busily planting rice:

> Looking over
> the spacious field spreading out
> with rice seedlings,
> I offer my heart-felt gratitude
> for the humble people's blessing

Women at Inns and Tea Houses

In large cities like Edo, Osaka and Kyoto, as well as at post stations, there were women working in the service industry and they drew the attention of female travelers.

Yamada Towako was intrigued by her encounters with women of the commoner class, who were working at tea stalls and inns in the post station towns on the way from Yamagata to Tatebayashi. She drew their poses and demeanor on many sheets of paper. At Namezu in Shichigashuku, where they took a lunch break, she was favorably impressed by the wife of the tea stall owner, a woman in her early thirties.

She was tall and pleasant looking, had her hair tied up modestly, and had easy manners. Although her attire was humble, her demeanor was polite and gentle. I would have loved to see her dressed in a fancy outfit, too. The woman showed exemplary courtesy. She reminded me of the *hokku* that my grandfather once composed, as he must have had pictured somebody like her in his mind:

> Free of vanity are
> the wild cherry blossoms—
> a genuine beauty

Oda Ieko and her party took a daytime tour to Shin-Yoshiwara, a licensed quarter in Edo, where they saw the courtesans' ceremonial procession, called the *oiran-dōchū*. She was astonished and greatly impressed by its splendor.

With large parasols held for them and each surrounded by a large entourage including a child apprentice, the courtesans paraded in and out the tea houses. Oh how beautiful they were!

> Just to see them
> makes your heart throb,
> those beauties—
> Why would people call them
> bamboo adrift on the river?

Courtesans are so beautiful and make us feel so happy. Why do we often regard them as "poor creatures adrift in the world"? It seems that Ieko was so impressed that she felt compelled to cast doubts on a common perception of the courtesans.

Nomura Bōtō-ni, the fifty-six-year-old widow of a retainer of the Fukuoka daimyo, came across harlots during her journey to Kyoto in 1861, when she was aboard a ship at Shimonoseki with her attendants. The girls approached even to Bōtō-ni, who had taken Buddhist tonsure. She wrote:

Small boats carrying harlots approached one after another, and the women solicited their services. What a wretched scene to witness. Our boat did not depart on that night, and there were only a few passengers left on board since most male travelers had gone ashore to enjoy themselves. Those women even came to ask me to buy them. . . . It was quite pathetic and sad, so I gave some money to three of them, pretending that I bought them, and let them leave. Then two girls of about twelve to thirteen years old came to massage my shoulders. I tipped them and let them go.

> Though there is
> none in this floating world
> who never suffers,
> sad are those who sell themselves
> to the boats floating in the port

Bōtō-ni demonstrates in this *waka* her deep pity and compassion towards these women, forced by circumstances to prostitute themselves to the boats' passengers.

NOTES

1. It was also to prevent daimyo from creating weapons caches in their Edo mansions; daimyo compounds armed with guns could be a threat to the security of Edo, the shogun's capital.

2. The custom is often believed to have come from the south, probably the Indonesian islands or the Malay Peninsula in ancient times. Until the medieval period in Japan, both men and women of the upper classes stained their teeth at the age of eight or nine as a rite of passage. That age was raised to thirteen to seventeen during the Tokugawa period, when women began dyeing their teeth around the time they married; dyed teeth now symbolized married women's chastity since black was perceived as an unchanging, permanent color. The custom had a practical purpose, too; namely, the solvent used for dyeing was a mixture of iron and tannic acid, which would protect the surface of teeth and prevent cavities and pyorrhea. Nihon fūzokushi gakkai, ed., *Nihon fūzokushi jiten*, pp. 71–72.

3. Here Shiba writes Imagire instead of Arai in the original text, indicating the term Tsū-jo chose to refer to the place in her diary. The Imagire area was a part of Arai at the time, and the names were apparently used interchangeably. I use Arai for consistency.

4. In the *waka* tradition "wetting one's sleeve" indicates tears from weeping or sobbing.

5. Here, in the original text, she is referred to as Saigusa Ayako; Saigusa was her maiden name, according to Shiba. Ayako probably used either Tsuchiya (her husband's surname) or Saigusa depending on the situation. In my translation I consistently refer to her as Tsuchiya Ayako. See note 2 of Chapter One about women's surnames at the time.

6. It was a *nakayashiki* (middle mansion). See note 101 of Chapter One for a further explanation of daimyo mansions in Edo.

7. *Bansho* were checkpoints daimyo created in their own domains, following the example of the *bakufu*'s *sekisho*. Their purposes and actual functions are discussed in Vaporis, *Breaking Barriers*, pp. 128–133. While they were officially different, it seems that people did not necessarily distinguish the usage of the two words.

8. The hole may have been installed by the domain to function as a byway for travelers without permit; if a human being crawls with both hands and feet on the ground like a dog, he or she would be "four-legged," therefore by definition not human, and could probably be overlooked by the guards.

9. Considered a defilement in Shinto.

10. The entertainers collectively referred to as *shirabyōshi* sang and danced to popular melodies, but sometimes composed and recited traditional *waka*, too. They flourished during the late Heian through Kamakura periods. In the case of female *shirabyōshi*, their professional activities sometimes involved prostitution. Nihon fūzokushi gakkai, ed., *Nihon fūzokushi jiten*, pp. 310–319.

11. A large-scale rebellion against the *bakufu* and domain authorities for their fierce taxation of the peasants of Shimabara (in Kyūshū), which lasted about five months in late-1637 to mid-1638. Since its leaders were mostly Christians, the *bakufu* started to enforce an isolationist policy and a ban on Christianity after they quelled the rebellion.

12. A monk (1415–99) of the True Pure Land Sect (*Jōdo Shinshū*) and the 8th head of the Kyoto Hongan-ji.

13. A residence Rennyo had built in Yoshizaki (in present-day Fukui prefecture) as a base for his efforts to spread the teaching of True Pure Land Sect. He simplified rituals and rewrote Shinran's (the founder of the sect) sutras into easy-to-understand

hymns. Rennyo's efforts bore fruit, winning many followers not only in the region but from northern Ōshū; the sect throve and a temple town was formed in Yoshizaki. Ueda and others, eds., *Nihon jinmei jiten*, p. 1442.

14. One of the founding members of the Meiji government and long-term ally of Saigō Takamori, though they later had a confrontation regarding foreign policy. See note 92 of Chapter One.

15. Army general and politician in the Meiji and Taishō periods.

16. There is some doubt about her age, notes Shiba in the original text.

17. A comprehensive work on his life and art is available in Lawrence E. Marceau, *Takebe Ayatari: a Bunjin Bohemian in early modern Japan*, (Ann Arbor: Center for Japanese Studies, University of Michigan, 2004).

18. One of the *Ōmi hakkei* (the eight beauty spots around Lake Biwa in Ōmi province); specifically night rain at Karasaki was considered beautiful, and the old pine tree there was also famous. Here Fuboku and Fuyū evoke rain and the pine tree for their verses, respectively.

19. As was mentioned in note 16 of Chapter One, it was customary to add —*jo* at the end of a woman's name as a courtesy; in her case both Rei and Rei-jo are used in Shiba's original text.

20. The first day of the Horse in the second month; the Horse is the seventh of the twelve animal signs of the Oriental Zodiac.

21. See note 86 of Chapter One.

22. The names of some one hundred places and the dates of her visits are listed in the original text, but omitted in my translation for readability.

23. Jūshin-in writes in her diary, ". . . it was the best among the local specialties we had tasted so far, but I was still hungry, so I requested something not sweet, . . ." Shiba, *Edoki no onnatachi ga mita Tōkaidō*, p. 244.

24. Here her diary is introduced as "*Shimazu Zuishin-in dōchū nikki*" (Travel journal of Shimazu Zuishin-in); this is simply another title for the "*Edo kudari nikki*" (Leaving Edo) introduced in "Travel of Daimyo Families" in Chapter One, according to Shiba, Letter to the translator, p. 3.

Chapter Three

Cultural and Philosophical Backgrounds

WOMEN'S EDUCATION

Learning at Home

Various schools were established during the Tokugawa period. First, there was the *bakufu*-sponsored academy, the Shōheizaka-gakumonjo in Edo, where high-ranking vassals of the shogun would enroll their sons. Then, there were over two hundred domain schools (*hankō*) across the country, founded by the domains for the sons of their samurai. There were also local schools (*gōkō*), opened with the permission of and supported by the domains for the children of both samurai and commoners. Girls were excluded from those institutions, except for a few local schools, and their education was generally left to their families.

Girls at the time were expected to train in feminine skills such as spinning, sewing, washing, and cooking, as stipulated in the precepts for women. In addition, they normally learned reading, writing, and literary arts at home, where mothers and grandmothers were often the major force behind their education. In some cases fathers and brothers trained them in the art of letters; moreover, experts in various fields could be invited to their homes to help further their education.

Ninomiya Fumi, the daughter of Ninomiya Sontoku,[1] began to learn writing with her brother when she was about seven; they were guided by both their father and his disciples. When thirteen, Fumi began to receive serious training in calligraphy from the expert Ōkubo Bunrin, her father's fellow scholar who often visited their home, and in painting and drawing from Ōoka Unpō, an Edo artist.

Naruse Isako, the author of *Karanishiki* (Chinese Brocade), a moral text
for women, received training in native-Japanese writing (*yamatobumi*) since
childhood from her grandmother Rishin-ni, who had experience serving at a
daimyo mansion; Isako's study was focused particularly on *The Tale of Genji*
(*Genji monogatari*) and *Essays in Idleness* (*Tsurezuregusa*), classical works
from the 11th and 14th centuries.

Kutsukake Nakako, the author of *"Azumaji no nikki"* (Diary of Traveling
East), was brought up by her grandmother after she lost her own mother at
the age of three. When she was five, her grandmother began to orally instruct
her in *Single Poems by a Hundred Poets* (*Hyakunin Isshu*),[2] all of which Nakako memorized. At the age of six, she began learning to write; then became
interested in *Teikashū* (A Collection of *Waka* by Fujiwara Teika) when she
was seven or eight. Reciting some verses from the collection, she began to
aspire to become a poet, according to her *"Oboroyo monogatari"* (Tale of a
Misty Night).

Education of the daughters of court aristocrats was focused on Japanese
classical literature and *waka*, according to a study of women's education
(*Joshi kyōiku shi*). They started to copy the introductory book of Japanese
hiragana syllabary and verses of *waka* at about the age of five; then would go
on to learn Chinese *kanji* characters by reading aloud and copying texts such
as *"Senjimon"*[3] and *"Keisho."*[4] Later they would familiarize themselves with
The Tale of Genji and other works of classical literature, also by reading them
aloud (*sodoku*).[5] Training in *waka* composition was normally the province of
experts. In addition, they studied various subjects, including ceremonial pro-
tocols, national history, calligraphy, painting and drawing, the art of incense,
flower arrangement, handicraft, and playing musical instruments.

Education of Samurai Daughters

Daughters of the samurai class, especially those of high-ranking retainers,
were educated in the fundamentals of women's virtues based on Confucian
ethics, including the three forms of obedience[6] and the seven grounds for
divorce.[7] In addition, they received further specific instruction as preparation
for becoming daimyo wives, should such an opportunity arise. Those instructions were normally written by grandfathers, grandmothers, parents, or other
elder members of their families.

Tōdō Ranko of the prestigious Tōdō family of Ueno in Iga province devoted her all-out effort to the education of her daughter Suma, for whom she
wrote an instructional essay *"Moshiogusa"*[8] as a wedding gift. The essay consists of forty-four headings including wifely duties, courteous treatment of
one's husband's mistresses and their children, kind treatment of servants, and

religious duties. "*Moshiogusa*" was copied and handed down from mother to daughter for generations.

Okaya Katsu, the daughter of a retainer of the Yamagata daimyo, lost her father early and was raised by her mother. Katsu, devoted to her studies since childhood, was said to have memorized the Confucian classics *The Analects of Confucius* and *The Sayings of Mencius* at an early age. After marriage, she enthusiastically engaged in the education of her three sons and two daughters. Her third son, Samanosuke, later became chief retainer of the domain, and distinguished himself by his achievements in its administrative reform. Her oldest daughter Towako familiarized herself with *waka*, *kyōka*, and painting and drawing, and her talents were well demonstrated in her travel diary "*Dōchūki*" (A Record of Our Journey). Katsu must have been the driving force and contributed a great deal to her daughter's education, since Towako never had a tutor nor joined a school for her studies.[9] Katsu wrote a few moral instructions for her grandchildren, too, one of which was a set of verses composed for her granddaughter; it is the "*i-ro-ha uta*" (equivalent to the alphabet song, with the initial letters of the verses matching those of the Japanese syllabary in their original order), a part of which may be translated as follows:

> Be always in a good humor and do not be rebellious
> Do not be argumentative
> Do not be angry and fight
> Calmly ask for others' advice
> Follow your husband in various matters
> Keep the house well during his absence
> Observe women's virtues

Such rhythmical verses were probably used as text for calligraphy practice.[10] Katsu, the educator in the family, was also a dutiful daughter, who nursed her sickly mother for a long time. She was loved and respected as an exemplary figure by her family members for many generations.

Temple Schools

Families of the commoner class were busy earning their livelihood and normally had neither resources nor time to properly educate their children at home. Farmers' daughters attended the village's girls' rooms (*musumeyado*) and needle shops (*ohariya*), where they learned from experienced housewives the social and industrial skills that were necessary to be capable housewives themselves in the future.[11]

In terms of reading and writing, oftentimes they learned at local temple schools (*terakoya*) or writing-practice halls (*tenaraijo*), which were typically run by Buddhist or Shinto priests, village masters, doctors, masterless samurai (*rōnin*), or women who had completed their service at samurai households. The number of temple schools increased during the closing years of the Tokugawa period, eventually numbering more than 15,000, according to a database of the history of Japanese education (*Nihon kyōikushi shiryō*) compiled in the first year of Meiji.

The data also indicate the existence of co-ed temple schools across the country and that a substantial number of girls studied in those schools. Suzuki Yoshitaka's study on female *terakoya* teachers ("*Terakoya onna kyōshi no kenkyū*") reports that Edo at the time had a total of 297 temple schools, 99 percent of which were co-ed, with the exception of two for boys-only and one girls-only. The study also indicates that 51 percent were co-ed nationwide, but the percentage is presumed to have probably been higher in reality. The enrolment rate of female students was especially high in large cities, which probably reflected parents' desires and expectations for their daughters to find opportunities to serve samurai families or to acquire the three basic skills necessary to work at merchant houses: reading, writing, and abacus (arithmetic).

Temple schools had female teachers, too. According to Suzuki's study, 174 out of the 15,652 schools nationwide listed in the database mentioned above were run by women, only a little over one percent, but more than three percent of all the teachers were women.

Some women ran *terakoya* that were much larger than those owned by men. Ariura Kinkō of Hita in Bungo province, for example, boasted an enrolment of 2,000 students in her Sansendō over a period of fifty years. Shortly thereafter, the renowned scholar Hirose Tansō opened his private Kangi-en academy in the region.

Kurosawa Toki was a woman who ran her own *terakoya*. In her childhood, she learned National studies and Chinese classics from her grandfather, who ran a seminary for mountaineering asceticism and a private academy. After being widowed, Toki returned to her natal home with her two daughters; then began making a living by peddling, while participating in meetings dedicated to the literary arts in various places to learn *haikai*, *kyōka*, and *waka*. Later on she settled down in her hometown and devoted herself to children's education. Fragments of her diary from that time still exist, in which Toki recorded her nineteen pupils' attendance (including boys and girls) and her other activities as a *terakoya* master; for example, washing the clothes of the children who fell into the pond, appeasing the girls fighting and crying, and helping her pupils work the fields. Her diary also records the vegetables and fruits that her pupils would bring in lieu of the payment of tuition, receipts of 100 *mon* for the monthly tuition, and receipts of 100 *mon* for the writing example sheets.

Some co-ed temple schools instructed boys and girls separately, perhaps assigning one group to the room upstairs and the other downstairs, or dividing their class hours into morning and afternoon. Kurosawa Toki's school reportedly used a *tatami*-mat room for boys and a wooden-floor room for girls.

Teaching materials normally used for girls were moral texts on women's virtues, filial piety, and basic instructions for commercial activities. For training in the art of literature, *Single Poems by a Hundred Poets* was a popular textbook.

Private Academies

There also appeared houses that provided education at a higher level than could the temple schools, though the distinction was not very clear-cut at times. Mostly taught at the residence of the educator, they were called private academies (*shijuku*); they offered courses in fairly advanced academic subjects and literary arts, in addition to Confucian ethics. Private academies emerged nationwide, and throughout the country women enrolled to learn the art of letters.

Among women of letters were those who had studied at private academies run by their fathers or husbands. Often, those women worked as teaching assistants, and later on ran the academies after their fathers or husbands had died.

Yanagawa Kōran of Sonemura in Mino province acquired skill in classical Chinese prose and poetry studying with her second cousin Seigan; the two of whom eventually decided to marry. He was a wandering poet, and she traveled with him to various places including Kyūshū and Bōsō, socializing with local literati for further training in poetry. She assisted Seigan when he opened a private academy Tamaike-Ginsha in Edo. The couple later moved to Kyoto, where they engaged in political activities. Seigan died just before he was to be arrested in the Purge of the Ansei Era. Kōran went to prison as his substitute. After being released she opened a private academy in Kyoto to teach Chinese classics. Among her students was Miwada Masako, the founder of Miwada Girls School in the Meiji period.

There were also women who, having served at the inner palace of Edo Castle or upper-class samurai households, came home and ran academies, thus contributing to the education of the local population. Some of them had originally been summoned for their academic excellence, and served as literary assistants or tutors; others had acquired literary skills from experts while in service. In either case, their work experience provided them with a higher education.

Tamura Kajiko, the daughter of a weaving-shop owner and trader of Kiryū in Kōzuke province, was summoned to Edo Castle as a calligrapher at the age of seventeen. She returned home when she was thirty-one years old and succeeded leadership of the family business with her husband, who was adopted into her family. At the same time Kajiko opened her Shōseijuku academy to teach *waka*, prose, and decorum. The academy prospered with over one hundred men and women enrolled. Among her students was Mochizuki Fukuko, who would serve the mother of the Sonobe daimyo in Tanba province as her literary assistant upon Kajiko's recommendation, and was later promoted to the lady's amanuensis. Fukuko resigned at the age of twenty-two, returned home, and succeeded Kajiko as teacher at Shōseijuku.

The number of women who ran private academies was at least as large as those who managed temple schools. Among them was the nun Chikan Zen-ni of Obuse in Shinshū, cherished by people as the "Granny-poet." She learned Zen philosophy, Chinese classical verses and the *ichigenkin* (a one-stringed *koto*-like instrument) from her Zen master Katsubun, who was the teacher of the renowned philosopher Sakuma Shōzan[12] and Takai Kōzan, the wealthy farmer-merchant and man of letters of Obuse. She also studied the arts of flower arrangement and tea ceremony from her master. After the death of Katsubun, she built herself a hermitage, supported by Takai Kōzan, in the precinct of his family residence. At her hermitage, called Sokushin-an, she taught local women calligraphy, poetry, *koto*, decorum, and tea ceremony.

Fujishiro Ichime, the daughter of a wealthy farmer of Kemigawa in Shimōsa province, founded a private academy when she was twenty-nine years old after divorcing her husband, who had been adopted into her family. She taught Chinese classics and calligraphy. The enrollees were said to have eventually numbered three thousand; an old roster that still exists identifies 1,274 students, one quarter of which were women.[13]

Unlike temple schools, many private academies continued into the Meiji period, when a number of new academies were also established by women, as well as men. Among them were some which evolved into high schools, colleges, and universities under the newly-introduced modern education system.

Options for Remote Residents

There was the option of correspondence learning, in cases where the student and the teacher lived far apart. When Ninomiya Fumi was young, her father Sontoku had Edo artist Ōoka Unpō send her example paintings so that she could copy them for practice and send them back to the master for feedback.

Unpō gave Fumi the pen name Kihō and rejoiced over his young disciple's steady progress, which he often mentioned in letters to her father. Fumi continued her correspondence study while working as her father's deputy at the *jin'ya* (an administrative office) of Sakuramachi in Shimotsuke province after Sontoku left for Edo with his son Yatarō.[14] She often asked Yatarō to obtain and send her writing examples for her calligraphy practice; then she sent her work to the masters in Edo for feedback. Fumi also received instruction from the calligrapher Ōkubo Bunrin, who gave her the pen name Shōrin, when he stopped by at Sakuramachi on his way to Edo.

Morimoto Tsuzuko and her husband received training in National studies from Uchiyama Matatsu, a disciple of Motoori Norinaga, and *waka* from Hattori Sugao and Takabayashi Michiakira. Tsuzuko had already been Matatsu's student in her days as a young maiden in Hamamatsu, and continued to learn from him after moving to Iida upon her marriage. They kept up correspondence via the pilgrims traveling to Mt. Akiha; she wrote her compositions and questions in a notebook, and the teacher entered in a margin of the notebook his feedback, critique, and explanations. After the death of Matatsu, the couple became students of Michiakira, who was Matatsu's leading disciple and also a student of Motoori Norinaga. During Tsuzuko's homecoming trip to Hamamatsu, Michiakira visited the couple, bringing fireflies he had collected as souvenir, and sojourned with them for three days to lecture on *Kokinshū*. Hattori Sugao also traveled often from his home province Suruga to the residence of the Morimotos at Shimada in Shinano, where he stayed for a substantial period of time and exchanged verses of *waka* with the couple and their fellow poets. He also visited the family to give lectures to Tsuzuko on *Man'yōshū*, *Kokinshū*, *The Tale of Genji*, and *Tales of Ise*.

Women would also participate in short-term schooling, so to speak; they visited their teachers at faraway locations, staying for a certain period of time to hear lectures or receive instruction in literature.

Hoashi Misato, the daughter of the Shinto priest Hoashi Nagaaki of Kubarumura in Yamaga (Higo province in Kyūshū) left for Kyoto and Ise with her parents in 1801, when she was fifteen years old. They first stayed in Kyoto, where Misato joined her father and his fellow scholars composing *waka*; then the family went on to visit Nagaaki's teacher Motoori Norinaga at Matsuzaka in Ise province, the main purpose of their travel. They rented a room in Matsuzaka; father and daughter commuted to Norinaga's place to hear his lectures and attend *waka* meetings. Though young, Misato was fully capable of, and did not shy away from, exchanging verses with the participants, including Norinaga's son Haruniwa, daughter Mino, and adopted son Ōhira. Their stay in Matsuzaka was only seventy days, but Misato's talent was recognized by Norinaga, who praised her, "Ms. Misato is only fifteen years old, but is so gifted in composing both prose and verse that she makes her elders feel humbled." Norinaga gave her the following *waka* as a parting gift:

> A young twig of
> white chrysanthemum, whose scent
> is superior to others'
> How I want to see its brilliance
> in months to come

According to her travel diary "*Tōkanshū*" (A Collection of *Tōkan*)[15] Misato and her father copied a few volumes of Norinaga's writings including *Koji-kiden* (*Commentary on the Kojiki*) during their stay in Matsuzaka:

I composed these verses on the occasion of returning *Kojikiden* to Master Mo-toori, which I had borrowed and copied.

> The light of jade
> buried beneath the land,
> Now I polish the venerable stone
> with a courageous mind
> to make it shine all over the world

> Creating landmarks
> to light the correct path for
> our learning,
> How valuable are the passages
> our master composed

It was her father's wish and his arrangements that made it possible for Misato to hear lectures from Motoori Norinaga, who was then at the height of his career as a scholar of National studies, compose *waka* with his leading disciples, and copy his *Kojikiden*. The entire experience, though for a relatively short period of time, must have been overwhelming for the young Misato, but at the same time an invaluable opportunity for learning.

Passion for Learning

All those opportunities would have been useless had women not had the enthusiasm for learning. The very fact that so many travel diaries were written by women indicates their strong passion for learning, which, more than anything, was the driving force allowing them to achieve their goals by overcoming various difficulties.

Hirose Tokiko was close to her two-years-older brother Tansō and shared a room with him in childhood; there she became familiar with the world of academics while listening to her brother receive lectures from his father. When Tokiko was sixteen, Tansō, who had been studying at the private Kameijuku academy in Fukuoka, gave up his studies and returned home due to illness. He recuperated there, but sometimes his condition would become critical, and no one would be allowed to see him. At the time, their parents were preoccupied and extremely busy with restoring the fortunes of the Hirose family; their business had once prospered enough to be a purveyor to various daimyo houses but had lately been failing due to their uncle's bankruptcy. Substituting for her parents, Tokiko waited on her brother day and night, but Tansō would not easily recover. Tokiko embraced the Buddhist faith under a priest from Higo province, who happened to be sojourning in Hita. She fervently practiced Zen meditation, wishing for her brother's recovery in exchange for her own life; she made a grand oath that she would become a nun to return the mercy of the Buddha if his life was saved. Perhaps thanks to her strong wish and daily practice, Tansō gradually recuperated. Later he would found the academy Kangi-en. Though he constantly battled with illness, he devoted himself to the education of three thousand students from across the country. Even after her brother's recovery, Tokiko's aspiration to take Buddhist vows did not subside. She finally left for the imperial residence Sentō-gosho in Kyoto to train as a novice under Lady Kazahaya-no-tsubone, a devout nun and lady-in-waiting to a retired empress.

Strong-willed women, like Tokiko, were not unusual among those who chose the path of academic training. Jion-ni, considered to be the first person to propagate *shingaku* (Heart Learning)[16] in Edo, was born into the *sake* brewing Shirai family of Yoshida in Ōmi province. She lost her mother when she was eight. For the repose of her mother's soul, she aspired to train as a Buddhist nun and left home against her father's objections at the age of about fourteen or fifteen. Seeking a master, she went to a nunnery, where she attended Zen meditation and practiced asceticism enthusiastically. While undergoing harsh training, she fell ill and had to rest for convalescence. It was at that time in Kyoto, when Jion-ni heard Ishida Baigan's lecture on *shingaku*, a movement to better society. She trained under Baigan, and eventually came to enlightenment, though she was bereaved of her master when she was twenty-nine years old. She decided to spread Baigan's teachings in spite of being sickly herself. She went to Edo in 1745, where she devoted herself to evangelizing the *shingaku*.

Arakida Rei-jo, the author of supposedly over four hundred volumes on sixty different subjects, had enjoyed reading both native- and Sino-Japanese books since childhood, influenced by her older brothers. She did not like training in feminine skills; however, her parents believed that academics were useless for girls, and did not allow her to receive formal education. But Rei-jo continued to listen to her brothers' reading practice and memorized their textbooks, such as the Confucian classics *The Great Learning*. A story has it that her oldest brother, impressed by her enthusiasm, once told her to read aloud the *Tales of Ise* and the Preface to *Kokinshū*, and found her able to read them fluently even though she had not yet begun learning to write.

Rei-jo started to practice writing at the age of eight and then studied *The Analects of Confucius* and *The Sayings of Mencius*. She liked to listen to her brother tell stories of soldiers and warfare, while she could not make herself interested in the practice of various feminine arts and skills that was forced on her when she was about twelve years old. After she was adopted by her uncle Taketomo at the age of thirteen, Rei-jo was able to devote herself more freely to her fields of interest, as Taketomo himself was a lover of learning. She was taught Chinese classics by her uncle, began to study *renga* (linked verses) at sixteen, and became a student of the *renga* master Nishiyama Shōrin at seventeen. After Shōrin's death she entered the circle of another master Satomura Shōteki in Kyoto. At the age of about twenty-four, she married Ietada, who was adopted as a member of the Arakida family. With Ietada, who was also a diligent student, Rei-jo frequently traveled the Kansai region and socialized with people of letters. Later, encouraged by her husband, she began to compose *kanshi*, and became a disciple of a Confucian scholar in Kyoto. With the assistance of Ietada, she became fully engaged in literary pursuits soon after she was thirty; subsequently she created works in the genres of historical tales, tales of court nobles, diaries, accounts of travel, essays, *haikai*, and *kanshi*. Rei-jo's love of learning came to fruition, through her own strong will and supported by the warm encouragement of her family, in the form of turning herself into one of the foremost female authors of early modern Japan.

INFLUENCES OF CONFUCIAN AND NATIONAL STUDIES

Confucian Studies

The morality system that most strongly influenced people's lives in Tokugawa Japan was Confucianism, which spread to every corner of society as both the ruler's governing philosophy and the fundamental principle behind people's moral concepts. Confucianism emphasized the importance of ethical relationships between lord and vassal, father and son, husband and wife, older and younger brothers, friends; its five cardinal virtues were benevolence, righteousness, propriety, wisdom, and sincerity. It exercised considerable influence on the culture and thought of the time. Mainstream academic learning at the time, therefore, was the study of Chinese classics (*kangaku*), centering on sources related to Confucian philosophy; naturally it was largely a men's world of learning, not surprising since academia at the time consisted principally of men. However, the door to the study of Chinese classics was not altogether closed to women; as Kaibara Ekken suggested in his recommendations for girls' education ("*Joshi o oshiyuru hō*"), "Let girls start learning native-Japanese syllabary (*kana*) at the age of seven, and let them acquire men's letters (*kanji*), too."

There were women who grew up in an environment that allowed them to familiarize themselves with Chinese classics. Hara Saihin, Kamei Shōkin, Ōta Rankō, and Inoue Tsū-jo were the daughters of Confucian scholars; Numata Kōsetsu and Suzuki Sairan had a scholar and a *kanshi* poet as fathers respectively; Ema Saikō, Yoshida Shūran, Shinoda Unpō, Matsuoka Shōkaku and Takahashi Shunkin were the daughters of doctors; Yanagawa Kōran, Doi Shōtō and Yamamoto Shōtō were married to Confucian scholar-*kanshi* poets. Often, their fathers educated them in the same way as they did their sons from their early years. In addition, private academies run by men did not have their doors closed to women, unlike formal schools founded by the *bakufu* or domains; therefore, women were able to enroll in the private academies if they wished, where the training began with the reading aloud of Chinese classics.

A number of women trained enthusiastically to become *kanshi* poets, earning recognition equal to their male counterparts. One of the supplementary volumes of a *kanshi* journal which Kikuchi Gozan[17] published in the years between 1807 and 1832, for example, includes works by sixteen poetesses, including Saikō, Kōran, and Saihin.

Confucian scholars and *kanshi* poets, such as Rai San'yō and Yanagawa Seigan, often accepted female disciples; in Hirose Tansō's Kangi-en, too, were enrolled two young nuns, Chihaku and Chisan from a Zen temple in Mino province, who traveled all the way to Hita to study.

Morita Mugen, considered the foremost female scholar of the Kansai region, studied at Fujisawa Tōgai's private academy from about the age of nine. When she was twenty-eight, marriage was proposed in *kanshi* by Morita Sessai, a friend of Tōgai's; she replied in *kanshi* and married him. Later on, the couple lived in various places along the San'yōji road, where they opened academies to teach local children and youth.

While we do find poetesses of *kanshi*, a genre that had long been regarded as a male domain, in various regions during the Tokugawa period, their number was still overwhelmingly small compared to those of *waka* and *haikai* poetesses. Often, *kanshi* poetesses were half-teasingly called "female masters" or "women scholars"; at the same time, however, people tended to regard their talents highly, perhaps more highly than those of women artists or *waka* poetesses. A Who's Who of Edo literati[18] published in 1837 provides, in addition to their names and caricatures of their faces, their talents measured individually in terms of how many years their achievements might last, as well as the overall evaluation of each author described in the form of *kyōka*. Among the fifteen female literati selected along with the male authors, it was the *kanshi* poetesses who received marks as high as their male colleagues:

> Hara Saihin (Confucian scholar): 1000 years
>> Flawlessly learned,
>> impeccable are both her
>> verses and prose,
>> Her brilliant handwriting
>> simply startles your eyes
>
> Takashima Bunpō (Calligrapher): 990 years
>> Well-versed in literature
>> but excellent in Chinese poems
>> and calligraphy, too
>> The boss of the cerebral types,
>> who made her name in Edo
>
> Shinoda Unpō (Confucian scholar): 900 years
>> Not at all
>> is she an ordinary maiden
>> of Edo
>> either in literature, or
>> in her power for action
>
> Takahashi Gyokushō (Confucian scholar): 900 years
>> Her creation of
>> poems and painting, neither is
>> inferior to any other,
>> Should she be called the
>> flower of Edo, the capital

Learning calligraphy and painting was one way to approach the world of Chinese classics, and a considerable number of *kanshi* poetesses demonstrated their talents in both poetry and painting.

The Four Masters of National Studies and Women Disciples

Among various academic developments, eighteenth century Japan saw great achievements in National studies (*kokugaku*), which inquired into native ways of thinking that had existed before Confucianism and Buddhism were imported into the country. There were the so-called four great masters (*yon ushi*) in the field: An early-Edo scholar known as Kada no Azumamaro, dubbed the founder of National studies, raised the awareness of old Japanese ways through his research into *Man'yōshū* and other ancient literature; his disciple and *waka* theorist Kamo no Mabuchi further developed the tradition and, in particular, endeavored to revive the poetic rhythms of *Man'yōshū*; Mabuchi's student Motoori Norinaga, who is considered to have brought National studies to maturity during the mid-Edo era, established the concept of *mono no aware* (lit., pathos of things)[19] based on his research into *The Tale of Genji*, wrote *Commentary on the Kojiki* (*Kojiki-den*), and left distinguished achievements in the study of Japanese literature and language; the late-Edo scholar Hirata Atsutane, who studied under Norinaga's son Haruniwa, endeavored in the interpretation and annotation of ancient Japanese history in *Records of Ancient Matters* (*Kojiki*) and *The Chronicles of Japan* (*Nihon shoki*), and wrote *Tama no mihashira* (lit., the true pillar of spirits) in which he explained the formation of the universe. Later, National studies evolved ideologically, combined with Shinto, and became a spiritual backbone for advocates of the restoration of Imperial rule during the tumultuous closing years of the Tokugawa period. The four great masters founded their own academic traditions respectively, followed by a large number of disciples including many women.

Azumamaro's niece Kada Tamiko, after being widowed, studied *waka* and *kokugaku* under her older brother Arimaro, who had been adopted by Azumamaro as his son. Later, she served the Tokugawa of the Kishū branch, where she tutored *waka* to the daimyo's wife and daughters. After retirement, Tamiko lived in Asakusa (in Edo), and was requested to mentor the daimyo wives of Tosa, Himeji, and Oka in *waka* composition.

Kamo no Mabuchi opened his own academy Agataijuku in Nihonbashi, and among his three hundred or more disciples were reportedly over forty women. In particular, Yuya Shizuko, the daughter of a merchant, Toki Tsukubako, the wife of a *bakufu* retainer, and Udono Yonoko, the daughter of a *bakufu* retainer, were renowned *waka* poets, who were called the three talented ladies of Agataijuku. Shizuko died at the age of twenty, but her "*Ikaho no michiyukiburi*" (Journey to Ikaho), an account of her travel with her mother, is widely read. Murata Taseko, a second-generation disciple of Mabuchi, also composed a travel diary, entitled "*Ikaho no nikki*" (Ikaho Diary).

Motoori Norinaga taught students from all over Japan at Suzunoya (the name of his family academy, which he also used as his pen name) in his home town of Matsuzaka, Ise. According to Suzuki Kaori of Motoori Norinaga Memorial Library, nearly thirty of his students were women and the majority of those women enrolled in his academy with their families. Most of them were locals of Ise or Owari, but some came from farther away, such as Okada Takeko, the wife of the chief retainer of Hamada domain in Iwami province.

Among the enthusiastic female disciples were also Tonomura Jugen, the wife of a Matsuzaka merchant; Ōdate Tami, a farmer's wife from Kida in Owari; and Araki Mino, the wife of a town councilor of Matsuzaka, all of whom became his disciples with their families. Norinaga's daughter Mino authored "*Mino sangūki*" (Mino's Pilgrimage to Ise); she also helped her brother Haruniwa, who had lost his vision. With his wife Iki, Mino transcribed Haruniwa's works, contributing a great deal to Haruniwa's achievements as a scholar. Both Mino and Iki were excellent *waka* poetesses.

On the roster of Hirata Atsutane's students are entered many women's names; among whom are the famous loyalist Matsuo Taseko of Ina, Shinano; Hara Sugako from that same village; and Baba Kikuko of Nakatsugawa, Mino.

Local Scholars of National Studies and *Waka* Poetesses

The four great masters of National studies had many disciples; some received instruction directly from them and others through correspondence. In addition, there were those who only had their names entered in the rosters. Whichever their method may have been, they became leading figures in National studies in their home towns and villages, where they taught their own students. National studies spread across the country through the increasing numbers of direct and indirect students of the four great masters.

Sugiura Kuniakira, the head priest of Suwa Shrine in Hamamatsu and disciple of Azumamaro, married Azumamaro's niece Masaki. The couple strove for the spread of National studies in Tōtōmi province and became pioneers of Hamamatsu culture. Masaki gave Kamo no Mabuchi his first writing lesson when he was eleven years old. She had her own collections of *waka*, such as "*Yado no ume*" (The Plum Tree in the Garden) and "*Yoarashi*" (Night Storm); she also authored "*Jōkyōkikō*" (Travel Home to Kyoto), a travel diary of her homecoming trip to Kyoto at the age of forty. Kuniakira hosted monthly poetry meetings to promote the art of *waka*, and lectured on *Single Poems by a Hundred Poets* and *The Chronicles of Japan* to further the study of the Japanese classics. Among the couple's female students were Mori Hanko, who was also a close associate of Mabuchi, Yanase Ritsu and her daughter Tami, among others.

Murakami Tadamasa, the court physician of Kariya domain in Mikawa province in the closing years of the *bakufu*, was a student of Norinaga's second-generation disciple Motoori Naitō. He authored various works including his own *waka* collection "*Hōroshū*" (Humble Hut Collection), anthologies and commentaries of *waka*, travel accounts, and many more. Tadamasa was also known as a book collector, whose twenty-five-thousand books are now stored as the Murakami library in the municipal library of Kariya. Families of National studies scholars often produced *waka* poets and Tadamasa's family was no exception. His mother Mishiko, wife Michiyo, and three daughters all composed *waka*; his daughter-in-law Yone had her *waka* published in *Meiji kashū* (Collection of Meiji *Waka*) compiled between 1875 and 1880, and his eldest daughter Fukami Toshino authored "*Hazakura nikki*" (Cherry Tree Diary), an account of her travel with the family to Kyoto, Nara, and Ise in 1861. On the roster of Tadamasa's students we find the names of ten women, including a seven-year-old girl. Tadamasa's circle of friends included the Kyoto poetess Ōtagaki Rengetsu, her close associate Takabatake Shikibu, and Sakuragi, the Shimabara courtesan who learned *waka* from Rengetsu. In the house of the present Murakami family in Toyota city are preserved letters, drawings, and paintings these women sent to Tadamasa, along with the earthenware tea pot and rice bowl that Rengetsu had crafted.

Itō Tsunetari, a Shinto priest of Furumon in Chikuzen province, was a student of Norinaga's disciple Aoyagi Tanenobu, and taught many students of his own as a leading figure in *waka* poetry in Chikuzen during the late Tokugawa period. Besides National studies, Tsunetari made important compilations of books on maps and geographical features; he authored a number of works including the voluminous *Dazai kannai-shi* (The Topography of Dazaifu). His achievements in the field of National studies and the work of his female disciples are discussed in depth in Maeda Yoshi's research. In addition to his private Furumon-shōgaku academy, Tsunetari taught at classrooms set up in several areas along the Onga River, such as Ueki, Ashiya, Kurosaki and Akamagaseki. Among his students there were reportedly at least seventy to eighty women whose poems were included in his *waka* collections.

According to Maeda's essay "Literary Activities of Women of Northern Chikuzen in the Early Modern Era," Tsunetari compiled a collection *Oka no agata shū*[20] in 1836, selecting from *waka* composed by his students; thirty-nine out of some two hundred seventy authors in the collection were women, amounting to fifteen percent in all. As each of those women had as many as eight verses selected on average, the level of contribution by women rose to twenty-five percent of the total number of poems, an indicator of the quality of their poetic skills.

Some of the female disciples of Tsunetari authored their own books[21] of which the following are examples:

Kuwahara Hisako of Ashiya
Waka collection: "*Shikinami no shū*" (Sets of Waves), 1844.
Travel diary: "*Futara mōde nikki*" (A Pilgrimage to Futara), 1844.

Hatano Yumiko of Kurosaki (Tsunetari's second daughter)
Travel diary: "*Yuhara nikki*" (Yuhara Diary), 1848.

Kuroyama Sumako of Ashiya
Travel diary: "*Itsukushima mōde nikki*" (A Pilgrimage to Itsukushima), 1859.

Abe Mineko of Ueki
Travel diary: "*Ise mōde nikki*" (Diary of a Pilgrimage to Ise), 1840.

Oda Ieko of Sokoino
Travel diary: "*Azumaji nikki*" (A Journey to the East), 1851.

Under the guidance of Tsunetari, these women of Chikuzen were remarkably active in their pursuits in the literary arts. They gathered to learn and compose *waka* at local classrooms where Tsunetari visited regularly as instructor. Many of them had their works selected for the *waka* collections he compiled for his students, and some were financially well-off enough to patronize the literary activities of the region, and travel extensively as well. Their experiences often culminated in the form of the authorship of travel diaries. These highly-motivated local women of letters are indeed an important factor to be noted when considering the intellectual and cultural activities of the Tokugawa period.

THE WORLD OF *HAIKAI*

Circles of Men and Women Together

The women of Tokugawa Japan were so intimately associated with *haikai* that Chiyo-jo, the *haikai* poetess of Kaga, might be the first name to come to mind when speaking of women's literature of the early modern era. It is not only that Chiyo-jo's works were easy to understand and appreciate, but countless women were in fact drawn to this form of art, through which they shared their experiences and enriched each other's lives. Naturally, enormous numbers of poems were composed by women; however, many have been lost and are as yet unfound.

In modern literature, which highly values individualism and uniqueness of self, the communal creation of *renku* (the traditional *haikai* sequence) has become somewhat devalued; whereas the initial stanza of *renku* has become an independent form of literary art, renamed *haiku*. Yet in the Tokugawa period, the sequential *renku* was still the major form of *haikai*. Early on, composition of a sequence of one hundred verses was common. After Matsuo Bashō established his style, however, a sequence of thirty-six verses, called *kasen*, became the standard form. A sequence may be a solitary composition, but could also be composed by different numbers of people, including a group of two (*ryōgin*), three (*sangin*), four (*shigin*), and so on.

Women, too, participated in the composition of *renku* from the early years. The Who's Who of female *haikai* sages (*Kokin haikai onna kasen*) edited by Ihara Saikaku in 1684 introduces thirty-six women with their names and portraits. Among them are several celebrity poetesses: the renowned calligrapher Ono no Otsū; Suzuki Mitsusada's wife Mitsu-jo; Den Sute-jo, known for her genius since childhood; and the talented courtesans Yoshino-dayū of Kyoto, Yūgiri-dayū of Osaka, and Hanadori-dayū of Nagasaki. Most of those women poets were followers of the gentle, smooth style of word play created by Matsunaga Teitoku, who had served Toyotomi Hideyoshi as his amanuensis. By the time the Tokugawa *bakuhan* system was firmly established, women had already secured their place in the world of *haikai*, and maintained their status in subsequent years, as is well indicated in a number of *haikai*-related publications of the time.

"One should not be on friendly terms with one's poetess fellows, nor should one need to accept them as one's master or disciple," is what has come down as a rule that Bashō reportedly laid for the itinerant training of *haikai*. The precept itself, though, indicates the existence of many poetesses and further that men and women poets were normally on friendly terms with each other. Bashō himself had a number of female disciples, as well. For example, a *haikai* collection compiled by Ōta Hakusetsu, one of Bashō's disciples and the village headman of Shinshiro in Mikawa, includes poems composed by sixty-six women of various ages and circumstances from the region, including entertainers (*shirabyōshi*) and young girls.

In Bashō's *haikai* circles were also Chigetsu of Ōtsu, a patroness who supported the poet's livelihood with her adopted son Otokuni; and Sono-jo[22] of Osaka, whose clean, innocent beauty Bashō could not help but praise in his poem "white chrysanthemum / not a particle of dust can / cloud its beauty." With them he occasionally joined circles for the composition of *kasen*, sequences of thirty-six verses.

There were numerous examples of women travelling to visit like-minded *haikai* friends to compose *kasen*. Men and women not only sat side by side for poetic creation but, remarkably enough, a couple who were not married nor in a romantic relationship could travel together for poetic training without being seen as immoral.

In 'group literature' *haikai*, the participants, whether men or women, would candidly exchange their poetic inspirations and sensibilities. It is interesting that this form of literature had its heyday during the Tokugawa era, when the teaching "Boys and girls should stop socializing with each other at the age of seven" was supposedly accepted as a norm.

Microcosms Created with Simple Words

Now what subjects did women choose and what microcosmic worlds did they create in their compositions?

> That green paddy field
> spreading out before me—
> how would I love to fall into
>   Tatsu of Nakajizō, *Arano* (A Desolate Field)

> A young seedling of chrysanthemum—
> I plant it lightheartedly,
> hoeing the alley busily
>   Shihaku of Tashiro, *Kiku no michi* (Chrysanthemum Road)

> Changing dresses for the season,
> how pampered am I, not to
> have to weave it myself
>   Sono-jo of Ise, *Sonofukuro* (The Pouch)

> No longer having to fix the hair,[23]
> my hands found home
> in the heat of a *kotatsu* (brazier)
>   Chiyo-ni of Mattō, *Chiyo-ni kushū* (Chiyo-ni's Collection)

> Thanks to being a traveler—
> I get to taste fresh dumplings
> and sweet soybean flour
>   Suiwu of Noshiro, *Moura michi no ki* (The Road to Moura)

> The winter moon,
> my heart wanders away to meet my husband,
> now on his way home[24]
>   Kasame of Edo, *Kasame kushū* (Kasame's Collection)

> In a young bamboo
> is there a joint which the bush warbler
> does not know
>   Ikkō of Takahashi, *Ayanishiki* (Damask and Brocade)

The above are a few works randomly selected from various *haikai* collections. In the seventeen-syllable format, the authors expressed their lives and thoughts with unaffected, casual diction. Their words, though simple and humble, offer us a window to complex layers of sensibilities; some depict vivid experiences in a vast landscape, daily activities, their appetite for food, while others contemplate their circumstances and life's changes; all of which are amazingly candid and unconstrained expressions of their feelings.

Many unknown women, not necessarily highly educated, thus created microcosms of their own. Through *haikai* they demonstrated that they too were creators of the culture firmly rooted in everyone's daily life, as yet unrecorded in history books. Men, too, respectfully shared their viewpoints with women and children through the creation of *haikai*, in which there were no lines of division based on gender, status, or age.

Charged with such a spirit, men and women often traveled together to compose *haikai*; the pair could be father and daughter, husband and wife, mother and son, or friends. Men and women contemplated their lives together, became keenly aware of their place in nature, and recognized that everybody was equal in front of the great unknown. Many students of *haikai* thus traced the routes of the great Bashō's journeys and sought to understand his spiritual world.

Vitality of *Haikai* Poetesses

Women who enjoyed *haikai* were not only lively in spirit but tended to be achievers in their practical lives. They worked hard; therefore they often had financial resources, which enabled them to publish collections of their works and travel to expand their circles of friends.

After being widowed, Chigetsu of Ōtsu continued to work with her adopted son Otokuni in their family business, dispatching post horses at the Ōtsu station. She also managed the household diligently as matron of the family. Located at one of the major post stations along the Tōkaidō, her house had many visitors including her *haikai* master Bashō and his followers, to whom she often offered accommodation. When Bashō died, Chigetsu had him buried at nearby Gichū-ji; then hosted *haikai* meetings on the anniversary of his death in subsequent years. Her devotion to the *haikai* master, who had been junior to her, was definitely made possible by her family wealth.

Sono-jo, whose grace was compared to a white chrysanthemum by Bashō, moved with her husband and fellow poet Ichiyū from their home in Ise to Osaka, where she became a professional *haikai* judge. After Ichiyū's death, she moved to Edo and succeeded his practice as eye doctor. Sono-jo indeed led a very active life. She took Buddhist tonsure, for example, changing her name to Chikyō-ni and participating in Zen meditations under the priest Ungo; she also remained active in poetic composition and related activities, one of which was the dedication of thirty-six cherry trees to the shrine Tomioka Hachimangū in Fukagawa. In 1723 she compiled a self-selected collection of *haikai* entitled *Kiku no chiri* (Chrysanthemum Dust); then published another collection *Tsuru no tsue* (Crane's Cane) to commemorate her sixtieth birthday. Sono-jo would determinedly bring to fruition whatever her mind conceived.

Many women published *haikai* collections; the first was Shihaku of Narada (Hizen) in 1700, whose collection was entitled *Kiku no michi* (Chrysanthemum Road). Following are further examples: Shūshiki of Edo, *Ishinadori* (Child's Play) in 1713, a collection to commemorate the seventh anniversary of the death of her late master Kikaku; Shokyū-ni of Kyoto (originally from Chikugo), *Sono angya* (The Journey) in 1763, a collection to commemorate the first anniversary of the death of her late husband Ukikaze; Kotoji of Kyoto, *Kasa no tsuyu* (Dew on a Hat) in 1775, a collection to commemorate an anniversary of the death of her late husband Bunge; Shiyō of Hiroura (Kishū), *Ichimegasa* (A Woman's Traveling Hat), a 1788 account of her travel to Yoshino; Seifu-ni of Hachiōji (Musashi), *Nanatose no aki* (Seven Autumns) in 1797, a collection to commemorate the seventh anniversary of the death of her late master Shirao; Tokushū-ni of Kaga, *Momoyadori* (Shelter under a Peach Tree) in 1804, a collection to commemorate the seventh anniversary of the death of her late husband Takakuwa Rankō; Tayo-jo of Sukagawa (Ōshū), *Asaka ichi* (Asaka Market) in 1817, a collection of *haikai* poets from various regions; Kiyo-jo of Sendai, *Wasurezu yama* (Unforgettable Mountain) in 1825, a collection to commemorate the third anniversary of the death of her late father Otoji; Sasao-ni of Hinatayama (Sōshū), *Kakihōshi* in 1830, a collection to commemorate the seventh anniversary of the death of her late master Otoji; Ōkei-jo of Edo, *Onna hyakunin ikku* (Single *Haikai* Poems by a Hundred Poetesses) in 1832, a collection of works of female poets before the advent of the Bashō tradition; and Kagetsu of Sendai, *Iwanesō* (Grass Around the Rocks) in 1853, a collection to celebrate her seventieth birthday.

It is noteworthy how actively women of the time engaged in various editing and publishing projects, which required considerable amounts of energy and financial resources.

NOTES

1. An expert (1787–1856) in agricultural administration in the late Tokugawa period. He was born the eldest son to an impoverished peasant family in Sagami province, and later succeeded in restoring the family wealth by working waste lands, eventually becoming the largest land owner in the Ashigara area. He devoted himself to relief work in farming villages in the Kanto region; in the meantime he was entrusted by the Ōkubo clan, the chief retainer of Odawara domain, and its branch family, the Uzu clan, with their financial and agricultural reforms. See Ueda and others,

eds., *Nihon jinmei jiten*, p. 1025. Sontoku is perhaps better known by his given name Kinjirō to school children in modern Japan, a figure used as an exemplary role model of industriousness; in many schoolyards there were bronze statues erected of Kinjirō carrying a bunch of firewood on his back and simultaneously studying from an open book he held in front of him.

2. A collection of one hundred *waka* verses believed to have been compiled by the 12th century poet Fujiwara Teika.

3. A text for learning one thousand characters in rhyme compiled in ancient China; a version of it was imported to Japan and apparently widely known among the literate by the eighth century. A comprehensive explanation and the full text are available in Nomura Shigeo, *Senjimon o yomitoku* (Taishūkan Shoten, 2005).

4. Collectively refers to Chinese classics on Confucianism.

5. This style of reading was commonly practiced as a method of training children in the rhythms of classic Sino- and native-Japanese texts.

6. Women were to first obey their fathers in youth, their husbands in marriage, and sons when widowed.

7. It says that wives who have any of the following seven defects should be let go: 1) those who don't obey their seniors 2) those who are barren 3) those who are lascivious 4) those who are jealous 5) those who have bad diseases 6) those who are gossipy and 7) those who steal.

8. A kind of seaweed that was used to collect salt. The Japanese expression denoting the act of collecting the seaweed (*kaki-atsumeru*) is homophonic to the verb referring to the act of writing (*kaki*) and collecting (*atsumeru*); therefore *moshiogusa* could also indicate letters and essays. Kindaichi and Ikeda, eds., *Gakken kokugo daijiten*, p. 1944.

9. According to the descendants of Towako, she never stopped painting and drawing until her death at the age of eighty three. Shiba, *Kinsei no onna tabi nikki jiten*, p. 25.

10. Copies of moral texts for women were often used as calligraphy examples, with presumably much less attention paid to their content. Tocco points out how the context of women's education changed considerably during the Tokugawa period; "*The Great Learning for Women* could not have had the same meaning when read by a young girl in 1865 as it had in 1730. For one thing, the presentation of the text itself was different, and the illustration that accompanied the text changed with contemporary fashions in illustration to appeal to new generations of readers." Tocco, "Norms and Texts for Women's Education in Tokugawa Japan," p. 201.

11. Anne Walthall's "The Life Cycle of Farm Women in Tokugawa Japan" in *Recreating Japanese Women, 1600–1945*, ed., Gail Lee Bernstein, pp. 42–70, provides insightful discussion and information about women of the peasant class.

12. A scholar (1811–1864) of Confucianism, and later of Dutch studies; among his disciples were Yoshida Shōin, Katsu Kaishū, and Sakamoto Ryōma. Naramoto, ed., *Nihon no rekishi*, p. 48.

13. The original Japanese text clarifies that the number was presented at a conference of the *Sohozu* association of Chiba prefecture.

14. At a time when Sontoku was working for the financial reform of the Uzu family. See note 1.

15. *Tōkan* means the hilt of a sword. One of the two *kanji* characters used in the writing of this word is homophonous with another *kanji* that denotes the meaning "return"; thus the word *tōkan* has come to imply "return/come home." Kindaichi and Ikeda, eds., *Gakken kokugo daijiten*, p. 1366.

16. *Shingaku* gave "moral and spiritual justification to commercial activity" and by doing so it "sought to rationalize the expedient pursuit of profit," according to Jennifer Robertson, "The Shingaku Woman: Straight from the Heart" in *Recreating Japanese Women, 1600–1945*, ed., Gail Lee Bernstein, p. 88.

17. A *kanshi* poet (1772–1853) from Takamatsu in Sanuki province; he received his education in Confucian studies at Edo and Kyoto. The journal he published was entitled *Gozandō shiwa*, which was "his standard-setting anthology-cum-commentary," according to Sato, *Breeze through Bamboo*, p. 1.

18. Its original title was *Genzon raimei Edo Bunjin jumyō zuke* (Life Expectancy of the Works of Living Edo Literati).

19. This sensibility is defined in various ways. "Pathos of things" is Ivan Morris's translation in *The World of the Shining Prince: Court Life in Ancient Japan* (New York: Kodansha International, 1964), p. 197. Another definition is the "deep feelings inherent in, or felt from, the world and experience of it," according to Miner, Odagiri, and Morrell, eds., *The Princeton Companion*, p. 290.

20. Meaning "A collection [of *waka*] in Oka no agata." *Oka no agata* is the name of the county.

21. They are in book form but handwritten, and not printed for commercial publication, as is the case with most of these travel diaries.

22. She often referred to herself as Sono-me instead of Sono-jo, and some scholars follow suit. They are two different readings of the same *kanji* characters.

23. Obviously the author Chiyo-ni is a woman who took Buddhist tonsure, and so had a shaved head; she no longer has to use her hands to fix her hair.

24. My English translation of this verse is more explanatory than the original; a more faithful translation is found in Sato, *Breeze through Bamboo*, p. 24, as follows: "Under the winter moon my heart walks this street and that" with the foreword for the poem "While waiting near the fireplace for my husband to return, I wondered how cold he must be on his way home."

Chapter Four

After the Journey

LASTING IMPRESSIONS

The Kindness of Strangers

Long after their journeys ended, female travelers would reflect back on travel experiences that had impressed them deeply. Those unforgettable memories enriched their lives thereafter, helping them further grow as human beings.

Arakida Rei-jo and her husband became lost after visiting Kokawa-dera, the third site of the Saigoku (western) thirty-three temple circuit, during their travel to Kyoto, Nara, and Osaka. According to her diary "*Hatsuuma no nikki*" (First Horse Day Diary), the couple wandered about the paths between rice fields for some time in a quiet countryside where not a soul was to be seen. They eventually came across a Kannon temple. Resting and sipping *sake* at a humble tea stall by the temple, they asked its owner the way to Iwade. The man, obviously of the lower classes, turned out to be extremely kindhearted and sympathetic; he volunteered to escort the lost couple to their destination. Greatly relieved and pleased, Rei-jo felt as if she had been bathed in the mercy of the Buddha, to whom she had just offered a prayer at the temple. Even the pouring rain did not bother the couple, fortified by their dependable companion. They enjoyed the walk while listening to the tea stall owner explain about famous sites on the way. When they arrived in Iwade, the man went out of his way to find lodging for the couple. Profoundly grateful to him for his kindness, Rei-jo and her husband treated him to *sake* and gave him parting gifts, feeling reluctant to say good-bye.

Tagami Kikusha-ni, in her diary "*Taorigiku*" (A Single Chrysanthemum), gives an account of her own experience being helped by strangers. After a visit to Zenkō-ji, she climbed alone into Mt. Obasute and was enjoying viewing the moon when a thunderstorm hit suddenly, causing landslides on the nearby hill. She sought shelter behind some rocks and ended up huddling there overnight, intoning the Buddha's name intently. A local man named Dengorō and his wife, who had witnessed Kikusha-ni walking into the mountains, were worried when she failed to return on that day. They searched the mountain for her, brought her back, and looked after her warmly at their house. Deeply moved by the couple's kindness, Kikusha-ni composed the following poem:

> In Ubasute,[1]
> the 'granny dumping' village, landed
> a pair of merciful nightingales

She remained grateful for their kindness throughout her life, writing, "Had it not been for their kind acts, I would not have had survived that day."

In the midst of the Boshin War, Koganei Yukiko wandered in the mountains, fleeing towards Yonezawa and Sendai with her three young sons in tow, as described in her diary *"Boshin no mukashigatari"* (Olden Days of the Boshin War). Unable to bathe for days and clad in thin cotton kimono, they trudged through the cold early winter rain, finally reaching the town of Tsunagi on the border with Yonezawa. It turned out, however, that the inn accommodated exclusively Yonezawa retainers and no one else. Hearing of their predicament, some retainers invited the mother and her sons into the building and offered a bath, and asked where they were heading. The men advised that they proceed to Yonezawa, a land with an abundance of river fish and farm products available. The first warm bath in the long journey of exile and the kind advice of the clansmen were true blessings for Yukiko and her children, who were on the verge of losing their sanity, burdened by their tribulations.

Awareness of Peaceful Society

Around the area of Koishikawa, there is a row of many beautiful daimyo houses standing side by side, all decorated with treasures from not only Japan, but Korea and China as well. The streets are busy with people coming and going. What a contrast from the mountain villages where I have been vacationing! The country is indeed rich and the people prosperous. During my journey I have not, even once, been exposed to any harm in spite of traveling in a small private party. I am truly fortunate to be able to live a peaceful life under the reign of wise rulers.

The above passage from *"Ikaho-ki"* (Ikaho Diary) by Nakagawa Man, the wife of the Oka daimyo in Bungo province, was written in 1639, nearly forty years after the Battle of Sekigahara. The author traveled to the hot springs in

Ikaho and Musashino, where she enjoyed viewing myriad plants and flowers. Rejoicing over her safe return to Edo, she affirmed the happiness of living in a peaceful country under the rule of the Tokugawa.

It was not only Edo, in fact, that enjoyed prosperity at the time. Most castle towns outside Edo were also remarkably prosperous, surrounded by fields producing an abundance of rice and various crops.

Yashiro Nokawa, who had long served at the Edo mansion of Shirakawa daimyo Matsudaira Sadanobu, returned to Shōnai-Matsuyama after her retirement. Observing various sites on her way, she felt deeply grateful to the Tokugawa *bakufu*. When the party crossed the Senjuōhashi bridge and passed Takenotsuka, there appeared before them rice fields ready for harvest. She wrote in her travel diary "*Tabiji no tsuyu*" (The Dew on the Roads):

Along the way, I could see farms and rice fields spreading out in front of us. Waves of rice seemed to blend into the clouds, quite an interesting sight.

> With the ears of rice
> bearing the sign of a year
> of abundance,
> the plants turned yellow
> in the autumn winds of Oda

To my left I beheld the view of Mt. Ontake of Nikkō. Thanks to the god enshrined there,[2] we, the people of this country are allowed to enjoy peace. There is nobody who would not be grateful for his blessing.

Nokawa had just parted with the people who had come to send her off, but obviously soon forgot her loneliness. She was overwhelmed by her gratitude to the late Ieyasu, the founder of the Tokugawa *bakufu*, for building the foundations of peace and prosperity.

Saisho Atsuko, in her "*Matsu no sakae*" (Prosperity of a Pine Tree), recorded her impressions of Kumamoto when she accompanied Sadahime as chief lady-in-waiting for her marriage procession from Kagoshima to Kyoto:

We arrived in Kumamoto at dusk. The inn was beautifully arranged and the streets neatly swept up, demonstrating the kind consideration of the lord of this province. I could sense the wealth of the fief. It was indeed auspicious.

She was impressed by the domain's prosperity, as well as its expression of respect and thoughtfulness towards the princess of another fiefdom.

Yamada Towako, too, could not help but be grateful for the era of peace, when she arrived in Tatebayashi from Yamagata. She wrote in her "*Dōchūki*" (A record of Our Journey):

All of us, young and old, were able to travel all the way across the mountains and fields with no difficulties. It was indeed thanks to the ruler of our country.

> Look up at our lord,
> Had it not been for his majesty's
> blessings
> how could we have traveled
> the long paths so safe and sound

It was an official trip necessitated by the transfer of their daimyo to another fief. Still, Towako felt deeply blessed that their journey over remote country roads was without any threat of danger.

Reflections on Life

Today, too, I saw many fields being turned over. Peasants kept on plowing the soil, clad in straw rain capes and hats to ward off the rain. I was humbled to see their hard labor. They are indeed the treasure of the country. Sitting in a palanquin, I, a woman of the samurai class, passed by them as if I had nothing to do with their work. I was ashamed.

Tsuchiya Ayako, as described in her "*Tabi no inochige*" (A Journey with a Writing Brush), saw farmers working the fields when she crossed the Ōi River, heading for Hamamatsu on her way to Sakai, her husband's new posting. The scene keenly reminded her of the class differences that allowed her to obtain food without hard labor. Her heart ached.

At temple Hōzō-ji near Akasaka, Ayako had the opportunity to see a display of articles that had belonged to Ieyasu; among those were a desk at which Ieyasu had practiced writing during childhood and torn-up clothing items he had worn at numerous battlefields. Observing them, she wrote, "I was always lamenting over and complaining about my own circumstances and trivial matters. How petty I was." She was moved to tears, imagining how selflessly and courageously Ieyasu fought to bring peace to the people of the country.

Yamada Towako was interested by various working class women whom she encountered during her journey, such as the wives of tea stall owners and serving ladies at the inns. She observed in detail their appearance, manners, and clothes. Through her observation, she was reminded anew that it was not necessarily a pretty face but correct, genial manners and polite language that made a woman appealing; especially as the wife of a samurai, Towako reflected, she herself should always maintain exemplary manners and attitude toward life.

METAMORPHOSIS AND ACTION

Independence from Family

For Hoashi Misato, an eight-month voyage with her parents at the age of fifteen was a major influence on her life thereafter, in spite of having been imposed on her by her father Nagaaki, who had prearranged the entire itinerary. They visited various friends of Nagaaki, sojourned at Matsuzaka to study under Motoori Norinaga, and socialized in the intellectual community. The young Misato absorbed considerable knowledge and learned about the lives of people of different regions, which certainly contributed to her growth as a person.

When Misato was twenty, her father adopted Oka Sadaaki[3] as his son, in order to marry him to his daughter. Sadaaki had reportedly been Nagaaki's disciple, and the newlyweds assisted their father educate his students. Five years later, however, the two left home. The rift between the couple and the father was presumably caused by Nagaaki's reproach of Sadaaki on a trivial issue. It was a rebellious act on the part of Misato, who had been raised with the expectation that she would be her father's prodigy. Perhaps she decided to have her own life independent of her father. Nagaaki composed the following *waka* four years after she had left him:

A wild pink[4]
I raised and cared for
with all my heart—
Where would it wander now
abandoning its home

The poem evokes in our minds the forlorn figure of a father, who yearns to again hold his treasured daughter.

Morita Sessai and his wife Mugen left Gojō in Yamato province, where they had spent some years as newlyweds, and began to frequently move to new places at people's invitations, assuming an itinerant lifestyle. The couple opened classes at Himeji, Kurashiki, Fukuyama and other cities, where they taught the local people and composed their own works of poetry. One day, Mugen and her husband had conflicting opinions on whether or not they should expel the chief instructor of their class who presumably had caused a problem. Angry at Sessai, who allowed the instructor to remain, Mugen ran away from home, leaving behind her fifty-four-year-old husband and seven-year-old son. Until then she had been a faithful wife, always staying by her husband; however, wandering from one place to another for nearly ten years,

Mugen had obviously metamorphosed into a woman who could take action on the basis of her own will. First she found temporary shelter at the home of Fujisawa Tōgai, her poetry teacher in her youth, and with relatives, and later made her living by teaching at a classroom she opened at Onizumi in Kawachi. Mugen was thirty-nine years old when she separated from Sessai. After four years, in 1868, when the era was changing to Meiji, she returned to her husband through the mediation of mutual friends. Sessai, though, died four months after they reunited, and Mugen ran a private academy, raising their child by herself thereafter.

Into Political Activity

A journey to Kyoto in 1861 profoundly changed the life of Nomura Bōtō-ni of Fukuoka. At the age of fifty-six, she finally realized her childhood dream of visiting the old capital. The main purpose of the travel was to meet her *waka* mentor Ōkuma Kotomichi to ask for his guidance in publishing the works of both her late husband Sadatsura and herself. At the end of the year, she sailed across the Seto Inland Sea, visited Kotomichi in his Osaka residence, and went on to Kyoto.

On the fifth day of the first month of the year there was an annual festival at the Imperial Palace, allowing the admission of the general public. Bōtō-ni joined the crowd, clad in a kimono she had borrowed from the wife of the inn owner for the occasion.[5] She was apparently struck by a deep admiration for the emperor, writing in her *Jōkyō nikki* (Journey to Kyoto), "Merely hearing the announcement 'Emperor's presence' was so awe-inspiring that I was moved to tears." From that moment, Bōtō-ni became consciously aware of her feelings of reverence for the Imperial family. Her diary abruptly ended there and nothing else was written until her return home six months later, possibly indicating that she underwent a serious transformation of thought and engaged in some important unrecorded activities during her stay in Kyoto. One can obtain a glimpse of those activities from a few *waka* verses she composed and a letter she wrote to a female disciple at home: "The situation has grown tense in the capital. Even a civil war may be imminent, indeed. I see daimyo and warriors come to this city from the provinces. The domains of Hagi and Satsuma have purchased the town houses around their estates, and in their expanded territories gather a number of clansmen without scruple." Bōtō-ni was concerned about the precarious situation in the capital, the seat of the Emperor she revered. She apparently approached a few individuals who were considered loyalists: the poetess Ōtagaki Rengetsu by whom she was given a *waka* as a gift, Takabatake Shikibu, another poetess, and Muraokano-tsubone, the chief lady-in-waiting of the noble Konoe family, who was then in seclusion at a hermitage.

Bōtō-ni had probably first aspired to make her living as a *waka* poet by publishing her works in Kyoto, but decided to return home after realizing how difficult that would be, learning that even renowned poetesses such as Rengetsu and Shikibu had to support themselves as craftswomen in pottery making and carving respectively.

After returning home, Bōtō-ni continued to associate with Imperial loyalists; among whom were Hirano Kuniomi of Fukuoka and Takasugi Shinsaku of Chōshū. She hosted those activists to sojourns at her mountain retreat.[6] In 1865 the Fukuoka domain ordered confinement of its loyalist faction. Bōtō-ni, who was also under confinement, was summoned several times for investigation but remained silent about other activists. The following *waka* was her answer to the investigators. Clearly, she is determined to dedicate her life to the cause and even prepared for her possibly imminent death.

> On my aging body
> will I accept punishment
> for my fellow fighters,
> It is my life and calling
> to lighten their burdens

In the winter, she was banished to the solitary island Himejima off Fukuoka, but was rescued the following year by men who worked under Takasugi Shinsaku; then she was given shelter at loyalists' residences in Chōshū. In the meantime, Satsuma and Chōshū formed a union to fight against the *bakufu*. Bōtō-ni stayed with the Arase family in Mitajiri, hoping to witness the united army's expedition to Edo for the restoration of Imperial rule. Seven days in a row she visited the Tenmangū shrine at Miyaichi, where she prayed for their victory, dedicating one *waka* verse every day. The verse she composed on the fourth day demonstrates that her conviction as an Imperial loyalist was no weaker than any male fighter for the cause:

> Though not one
> am I to draw a catalpa bow
> like the soldiers,
> my devotion travels straight
> and as fast as an arrow

Her condition deteriorated around that time. She was sick in bed when the news reached her that a secret Imperial order was issued on 10.14 for the overthrow of the Tokugawa *bakufu*. Bōtō-ni died in the eleventh month of that year at the age of sixty-two, one month before the Restoration of Imperial Rule was proclaimed. She had believed in the coming of Imperial rule until the end, as implied in her farewell *waka* in *Bōchō nikki* (Bōchō Diary):

> Having awaited
> through a long winter confinement,
> all of a sudden
> spring seems to have arrived with
> all the flowers bursting out blooming

Becoming a Loyalist

Matsuo Taseko was fifty-one years old when she encountered the loyalist ideology of Iwasaki Nagayo, who happened to be visiting the neighboring town of Iida at the time; he was a scholar of National studies and a disciple of the late Hirata Atsutane. Taseko was deeply inspired by Nagayo and became a student of Atsutane's ideas. Until then she had led an ordinary life as the wife of Matsuo Junsai, the village headman of Tomono in Ina, Shinano province: she was loyal to her husband and parents-in-law, devoted to the education of their two sons and four daughters, focused on household management, farming and weaving, and looked after their servants well. In her youth, Taseko spent some years at a relative's family as a live-in student of manners, while studying at temple school and training in feminine skills in general. Later she studied *waka* with the Iida poet Fukuzumi Seifū.

Her husband Junsai was of a delicate constitution; the couple therefore traveled together often, partly for his convalescence and partly for recreation. For example, in 1845, when Taseko was thirty-five, they went on a pilgrimage to Zenkō-ji and Gochi-Nyorai (The Five *Dhyani* Buddhas) for half a month. Two years later, they visited Akiha Shrine, and then called on Ishikawa Ihei, who had succeeded the late Seifū as Taseko's mentor in *waka*. In 1855, when she was forty-five, Taseko and Junsai traveled to Edo for sightseeing with their fourth daughter and a relative. While in Edo, she had the honor of being invited to present her *waka* at the residence of their daimyo Matsudaira Yoshitatsu. They stopped by at Zenkō-ji again on their way home. In the summer of 1859, the couple went to the hot springs of Kusatsu in Kōzuke province for Junsai's recuperation. Their return trip included a visit to Zenkō-ji and the house of Matsuzawa Yoshiaki in Suwa, the itinerant merchant and scholar of National studies, where they visited with his wife.

Her travel experience had provided Taseko with opportunities to associate with *waka* poets and scholars of National studies in various regions; those journeys had broadened her knowledge and raised her awareness of the rapidly changing world. It was around that time that Iwasaki Nagayo was inciting people to patriotism with his lectures on National studies, *waka*, and the *nō* drama; Taseko, for one, became intensely concerned about the welfare of the country with the recent arrival of foreign ships off the coast of Japan.

In the eighth month of 1862, fifty-two-year-old Taseko left for Kyoto, the old capital that had then become a center for radical political movements; many samurai were gathering from across the country, including those who had abandoned their status as clansmen. For Taseko, too, this journey was purely of a political nature.

Once settled in a rented house at Fuyachō through the good offices of the wealthy merchant Iseya, she, as a *waka* poet, began to closely associate with groups of Imperial loyalists, among whom were court aristocrats, samurai activists of Chōshū and Satsuma, and the *waka* poetesses Ōtagaki Rengetsu and Takabatake Shikibu.[7] Taseko's lodging always had visitors who would bring "secret tasks" to be taken care of. In her diary during her stay in Kyoto are passages such as, "The landlord came to inquire about a certain confidential matter, so we went out together," "I was asked to carry out a secret task," and "I went clandestinely to a place called Uzumasa for a secret inquiry." Among her many "secret activities" is an anecdote in which she saved the life of Iwakura Tomomi,[8] whom radical loyalists considered a traitor due to his advocacy of a union of the Imperial Court and the Tokugawa shogunate. While they were attempting to kill him, the story has it, Taseko made the acquaintance of the Iwakura family, succeeded in meeting Tomomi, found him a moderate but ardent loyalist, and finally dissuaded the radicals from assassinating him.

She spent New Year's in Kyoto, offering congratulations to the Emperor and mingling with the ladies-in-waiting at a court banquet. In that year, activists of the Hirata school were arrested by the *bakufu* on suspicion of allegedly masterminding a certain incident that took place in the second month; someone beheaded the wooden statues of the first three rulers of the Ashikaga shogunate[9] enshrined at Tōji-in temple and gibbeted the wooden heads at the dry riverbed of Sanjō,[10] implicitly accusing the Tokugawa shogunate of being traitors. Taseko, who was suspected of involvement in the crime, was sheltered in the Kyoto residence of the Chōshū domain for some time.

There, she had opportunities to discuss national affairs with the clansmen,[11] and was given a dagger with a white scabbard by the Chōshū daimyo Mōri Takachika in a gesture of praise for her heroic loyalty. After hiding for about a month and a half, Taseko left the capital with her oldest son Makoto, who had come to escort her for her return trip. Stopping at the shrines of Ise and Atsuta, they arrived home in the fifth month. It had been nine months since she had left for Kyoto, where Taseko accomplished an important duty as a mediator for the Imperial loyalists. The accounts are recorded in her *Jōkyō nikki* (Journey to Kyoto).

Back home in Tomono, Taseko continued to look after those who would travel to the village counting on her support and assistance; often, they had escaped the *bakufu*'s pursuit or were involved in ambitious plots. She sheltered them on the second floor of her house, or in a hideout she arranged in the neighborhood, providing them with food and the bare necessities: rice, salt, *miso*, soy sauce, vegetables, firewood, charcoal, and so on. At times she even prepared clothing for them, gave them money for their exile journey, and secured safe destinations for them. Reportedly, there were always several activists staying at her house and the hideout nearby. Taseko's wholehearted devotion to the loyalist cause must have won the sympathy of her family members, and her activities would not have been possible without their full support. Her eldest son, Makoto, was once summoned to Edo for investigation for allegedly being in secret contact with Chōshū; the suspicion had arisen out of the arrest of an activist whom the Matsuo family had once sheltered. Still, Taseko continued to help the activists, never yielding to external pressures.

In 1868, when the Restoration of Imperial Rule was issued, Taseko went to Kyoto again with Makoto. She was received by the Iwakura family as their guest, later she and their lady-in-waiting Umeno (later Miwada Masako) were entrusted with the education of their daughters; Taseko taught them *waka* and Japanese literature in general. At the same time, she played an important role as a contact between activists and Iwakura Tomomi, earning the firm confidence of his wife Makiyama as well. Taseko was indeed an indispensable character in the Iwakura family story for over ten years stretching before and after the Meiji Restoration; she was called "the female councilor of the Iwakuras," and even nicknamed "the granny broker at the Iwakuras." Through her mediations, many activists later assumed administrative positions in the new Meiji government. During the Boshin War, when the eastern expedition army was formed, she had her eldest son Makoto serve in General Sawa Tamekazu's corps for the pacification of the Ōu region, and her second and fourth sons under General Iwakura Tomosada (Tomomi's second son) in the Tōzandō region. She composed this *waka* to celebrate the departures of her sons:

> Beat off
> the thorns and weeds of
> Michinoku,[12]
> Put on the shining brocade
> of beautiful flowers instead

After the dawn of Meiji, Taseko traveled to Tokyo in 1869 and 1881, where she once again engaged in mediation activities while sojourning at the house of Iwakura Tomomi, who was now a high-ranking statesman in the new government.

DIARIES THEY LEFT

Why They Wrote

Currently, there are close to two hundred travel diaries gathered in front of me;[13] the number is certain to grow as this research continues. Included in my ongoing search are some whose titles have been known to me for some time but, as of yet, not their whereabouts.

The purpose of the writing of travel diaries was, most likely, twofold: for themselves and for others. Certainly, the authors wanted to preserve the memories of their valuable experiences for themselves. It is a great pleasure for anyone to recall, through reading, deep impressions of past experiences.

Tozawa Mizuko recorded her sightseeing trip to Enoshima and Kamakura in 1821, when she enjoyed collecting seashells on the beach, an island tour in a small boat, and the vast landscape of mountains and ocean. At the end of her diary "*Tabi nikki*" (Travel Diary), she wrote:

> I did not write this to show it to others, but just jotted down various details of my experience for myself to remember in the future. However, this diary may happen to be exposed to others some day, and I feel embarrassed about my humble handwriting, unrefined diction and style. Furthermore, the excursion was simply for my personal pleasure, which must be quite insignificant for anyone else.

Yuya Shizuko concluded her travel account "*Ikaho no michiyukiburi*" (Journey to Ikaho) as follows: "Thus I have written in detail about my travel, which may sound quite trivial to others, but I heard it comforting to read later one's own writing on her experiences."

There are also practical purposes that motivate the traveler to keep a journal for herself; it helps her remember the itineraries, destinations, daily expenses, and other relevant facts such as donations of copied sutras to temples. Among the writings I have collected, in fact, are included some which have only simple words and numbers jotted down. Even from these terse memos, we can still learn various aspects of people's lives at the time; it must have been the same with the authors, too, who probably could recall later many memories buried behind those simple words and numbers.

Some wrote travel diaries consciously expecting readers other than themselves, such as their children, grandchildren, and those who could not experience travel themselves for one reason or another. Journeys for poetic composition were normally recorded for others to read, or for receiving their mentors' feedback; those works, therefore, were often rewritten many times, with slightly different versions existing as a result. Records of hardship, like those during the Boshin War, were also written to be read by others for generations to come.

How They Were Handed Down

Naturally, it has been through many people's efforts that we are now able to read these women's travel diaries, which have survived hundreds of years.

How they were handed down varies depending on the circumstances of each. Some were published via wooden blocks, others preserved in original form deep in warehouses for generations; there were also manuscripts that were copied by hand at different times. But in general, unlike in our contemporary society, writings by women were seldom kept in public institutions nor were they taken seriously enough at home for permanent preservation. Many of those that have survived are either by luck or resulting from certain individuals' special efforts. Otherwise, they could have been thrown away or burned as trash; actually many have been burned or gone missing over the years. In some cases, those writings had been carefully preserved until a certain generation by the descendants, but were disposed of by subsequent generations due to the renovation of their houses or for other reasons. I have encountered many times writings that had long been forgotten in people's warehouses; such encounters, for me, were not just the discovery of texts, but rather meetings with the very women who had authored the diaries. Among them are, for example, Morimoto Tsuzuko of Iida (Nagano prefecture), Orimoto Kakyō and Inamura Kiseko of Futtsu (Chiba prefecture), and Setoshi Oiwa and Okano of Gobō (Wakayama prefecture). Moreover, I found that some number of works, though preserved in libraries, had never been read or checked out. Kuroda Tosako's "*Ishihara-ki*" (Journal of Our Days in Ishihara), Ogasawara Iseko's "*Kisaragi no nikki*" (Kisaragi Diary), and Nakamura Ito's "*Ise mōde no nikki*" (Diary of an Ise Pilgrimage), for instance, had never been checked out, apparently, in spite of the substantial quantity and respectable quality of their texts. There are also collections of *waka* that carry the titles of minor travel diaries whose authors' names are missing; one such case is "*Hengyoku-shū*" (Collection of Jade Pieces) compiled by Tsumura Sōan, a *waka* poet and supplier to the Satake clan.

Travel diaries that were originally printed on wooden blocks are small in number as compared to collections of *haikai* and *waka*. But once published, they naturally became more visible and accessible; thus a few dozens of them were reprinted with movable type during the Taisho period (1911–1925).

Those that have been copied by hand often show discrepancies between different versions, posing difficulties for research into their contents. On the other hand, however, they are the most interesting; comparing several versions, one may find some parts arbitrarily revised, unintelligible parts rephrased with easy expressions, the same word transcribed in different characters, or certain lines deleted. Often, a handwritten copy has both afterword and signature by the person who copied; added to those are clarifications of the individual from whom the original was borrowed and the time it was copied, and sometimes the copyist even volunteers commentary or critique of his or her own. These afterwords could sometimes be an independent source for us to discover events and situations unrecorded elsewhere.

Significance of Travel Diaries

Simple records of expenses, destinations, lodgings, and itineraries were probably jotted down casually in small notebooks the women carried in their travel attire; cash books may have been made into clean copies later, though, should there arise the need for submitting them officially. Some of the diaries I have collected are indeed notebooks small enough to be carried in an inside pocket; among those are Matsuo Taseko's "*Miyako no tsuto*" (Souvenir from the Capital), Aoyama Toyo-jo's "*Zenkō-ji dōchū nikki*" (A Pilgrimage to Zenkō-ji), Setoshi Oiwa's "*Tabi nikki*" (Travel Dairy), Nakayama Miya's "*Tabi nikki*" (Travel Diary), etc. Those booklets certainly evoke the actual flavor of travel.

Some diaries were written soon after the author had returned home, while others were drafted five or even ten years after the actual journeys. There are also those that show the feedback from or corrections by their mentors in red ink. From various conditions of the diaries we are able to infer the circumstances under which the work was originally composed.

For the contemporary reader, their travel accounts provide a rare opportunity to approach the emotions and thoughts of these early modern women. We also discover various aspects of the society of the time through their lively depictions of local products, lifestyles, events, customs, scenic sites, shopping, souvenirs, and even the configurations of inns and temples.

For the author, writing a travel diary was to trace her own experience in words, and in drawings, to etch it on her memory with a vividness that she would never have been able to obtain through reading guidebooks only. Writing was also an act of reflection, through which the author could further mature as a person. Especially, drafting travel diaries with poetic compositions was a part of literary training; many of them, therefore, were written and rewritten.

As I have mentioned repeatedly, the records of those individual journeys, which must have enticed their contemporary readers with travel's allure, are at the same time invaluable sources for historical research into not only literature, but also various fields including transportation systems (both land and marine), landscape, tourism, food, and folklore.

EPILOGUE—A SUMMARY

Comparison with Contemporary Travel

Now I have traced the journeys of various women during the early modern era. With them, in my imagination, I have walked highways and crossed ridges and rivers. At times we were lost in the mountains, struck by storms, and even became seasick, but we also appreciated beautiful landscapes to our hearts' content. We did not attempt to go against nature; instead we followed the will of nature, waiting for favorable winds on the sea or for the water level to recede at rivers. We came across farmers working the land, merchants trading commodities, and women serving at tea stalls and inns; some women were even rowing tiny boats by themselves to sell fish. We imagined what their lives were like; at times we experienced surges of emotion, mixed with sympathy for their difficult circumstances and deep appreciation of their hard work. Visiting noted places of historical interest, we offered prayers and recited old poems, while reminiscing on old stories and thinking of our ancestors. Those were all invaluable opportunities for me to reflect upon myself, too.

While traveling, women could not simply follow the path of feminine virtue prescribed in moral textbooks of the time, but had to become more flexible and resourceful. They sat together with men to compose poems, climbed mountains hand in hand, lay down on the same floor of a boat, and spent days together in small crowded rooms during the civil war; the young and old, men and women, all shared meager food and drink while encouraging each other by the fire.

It was not uncommon for women to travel with friends of similar taste, but perhaps there were even more women who traveled with their families. Both the Confucian scholar Rai San'yō and the loyalist-activist Kiyokawa Hachirō invited their mothers to travel with them, well-known examples of mother-son pairs. Ordinary women, too, enjoyed traveling with their fathers, sons, or husbands. Indeed, many married couples traveled together. Our attention is drawn to those among them in particular who shared interests in academic learning or literary arts, such as *kanshi* and *haikai*. Together they would admire the moon, compose verses, and at times dedicate their poems at shrines and temples. A husband would look after his wife if she had difficulty in walking, holding her hand or carrying her on his back. They would walk dangerous paths together, avoiding checkpoints that were especially strict on women. Later they would share their experiences anew by either co-authoring travel diaries or drafting accounts independently. In traveling there was a world of equal relationships between men and women, husband and wife, and parents and children, deviating from precepts offered in the Confucian moral texts of the time.

As we have observed in reading their diaries, women greatly expanded their world through travel, developing relationships with friends, acquaintances and strangers alike. Among those strangers were villagers who let them stay at their places, people with whom they happened to travel together, and those who lodged at the same inns as they did; or they could be tea stall owners, palanquin bearers, skippers, and even daimyo, who spoke with them as equals at poetry circles.

Nature was a source for literary inspiration. It offered travelers real sounds, smells, and excitement, all of which were valuable source material for poetic composition, of a depth perhaps impossible in uneventful daily life at home. For that matter, making a journey at that time challenged people in deep, profound ways that may have been largely lost in our contemporary travel experience.

Comparison with Men's Travel Diaries

We have access to countless travel diaries written by men during the Tokugawa period; their writings have been much better preserved than those by women. Men, too, traveled for learning and training, but often their travel experiences had a certain aspect of recreation that was absent from those of female travelers; men's journeys often included activities with prostitutes and wild parties after the pilgrimage, or at the end of a term of abstinence in holy mountains. Women, on the other hand, valued and enjoyed the journeys themselves.

Many men had opportunities to travel in connection with their official duties. There were retainers who followed their daimyo in alternate attendance or transfer of fiefdom. Some samurai traveled due to their newly assigned positions and others were dispatched to various types of tours of inspection.

A number of men traveled for training in swordsmanship. There were researchers who went to explore geographical features, medical scholars who traveled to collect medicinal herbs, and professional writers and artists who traveled for the sake of collecting materials and creating their art works. Merchants traveled for trading. Their travel diaries, therefore, are different in various aspects from those written by women.

Women's Lives Reflected

From their writings, we often learn of the authors' lives beyond their travel experiences. For example, there were fathers and brothers who placed high academic expectations on their daughters or sisters, providing them with opportunities to further cultivate their talents, irrespective of the conventional social norms for women. The same was true for married women; it was not unusual that a husband, devoted to furthering his wife's talent, would travel with her to mingle with intellectuals and artists. In some cases a man would invest his entire fortune to allow an itinerant life with his wife for her learning.

We also saw women who lived their entire adult lives as travelers without any male supporters. Some traveled not for themselves but for their late fathers, husbands, or mentors, commemorating and further developing the achievements of the deceased.

There were women who left home, abandoning their parents, children, and even husbands, to live their own new lives in traveling.

Statistically, those in their fifties were overwhelmingly large in number among the women who took to the road, probably because many of them had either handed over their role as homemaker to the younger generation, or had been widowed and therefore were free of family duties. Finally able to live lives of their choosing, many likely desired to devote themselves to something new. Perhaps they had taken basic lessons in various forms of art and literature as young maidens, had never lost their passion for learning, and now in their fifties decided to resume their studies to enrich the remainder of their lives. Their positive and active attitudes towards life are indeed inspirational for us.

Women with Economic Resources

Clearly, women of the time did not necessarily spend their entire lives engaged only in household management and other domestic chores such as weaving, sewing and child rearing. Their writings indicate that they had financial resources, too. The cost of their travel must have been substantial, considering their journeys often took days and months and required attendants who would carry their luggage; in addition, their cash books indicate that travel of the time required various expenses that our contemporary journeys do not. Many travel diaries were written by women who had led their households and businesses; they had earned money, working together with their husbands for many years. Among the authors were also women working away from home, so to speak, who served as tutors or ladies-in-waiting at the homes of daimyo or other wealthy people. Whatever the form, many women had their own economic resources.

Slices of History

In a journal kept by the wife of a samurai we saw a vivid human drama that arose from a daimyo transfer. Chaotic situations were experienced by commoners and samurai families alike. We learned how they cared for a longtime pet, about their visits to their ancestors' graves, and what their temporary residence was like before moving. The journal also describes how the administration of a castle was transferred from one clan to the other, and how women and children journeyed to the new fiefdom of their domain lord. Those are all absent from history textbooks in general, which tell us only about socio-political systems and formal events.

Some diaries provide portrayals of women who became deeply involved in political activities during the closing years of the Tokugawa *bakufu*, some of whom spent time as captives away from home. Their writings often reveal otherwise unknown historical facts; for example, how ordinary people struggled to survive or even risked their lives to help others.

Similarly, among the facts that are barely elucidated in the official histories is the story of the women of the inner quarters of Edo Castle who contributed to its bloodless capitulation. Reading a travel diary kept by a lady-in-waiting we understand that many women were actively involved in efforts which changed the course of history.

On the other hand, travel diaries could occasionally reveal sad, painful aspects of life as well; there existed individuals who ran away from home for various reasons and disappeared in the darkness of history.

Through traveling, people expand the radius of their activities substantially; consequently the records of their journeys offer us a window to their lives on a far larger scale than do conventional diaries kept at home, discussing topics as varied as architecture, transportation, politics, economy, literature, and many others. For these reasons, I believe it a truly meaningful task for us to search and preserve those works and transmit them to the next generations.

NOTES

1. A pronunciation variant of Mt. Obasute. Obasute or Ubasute literally means "abandoning an old woman." The folktale *Obasuteyama* (Mt. Obasute) is a story of a son who, following the custom of the region, carries his aged mother to the mountain to let her die, but profoundly moved by her deep, unconditional love for him, brings her back to the village, determined to keep his mother until her natural death.

2. Referring to Tokugawa Ieyasu.

3. The *kanji* used to write his name could also be read Sadasuke or Sadakatsu. The intended reading is unclear. Shiba. Letter to the translator, p. 4.

4. The Japanese name of the flower is *nadeshiko*.

5. Bōtō-ni probably was traveling in humble nun's attire and needed an appropriate outfit for the auspicious ceremony. Her given name was Moto, and she took religious vows after her husband Nomura Sadatsura died.

6. A four-bedroom cottage that Sadatsura built in Mt. Hirao, partly for his wife so that she could concentrate on her poetry composition. Koishi Fusako, *Runin Bōtō-ni*, pp. 77–78.

7. In the Japanese original text are listed more people with whom Taseko associated in Kyoto: The court noble poets Ōhara Shigetomi, Shirakawa Sukenori, and Uratsuji Kimimoto; Fukuba Bisei of Tsuwano, who was a lecturer to Emperor Kōmei; Odamura Bunsuke (the later Katori Motohiko), Shinagawa Yajirō, and Kusaka Genzui of Chōshū domain; and Nakamura Hanjirō of Satsuma domain.

8. A court noble politician (1825–83) during the end of the Tokugawa through early Meiji era.

9. Ashikaga Takauji founded the Muromachi *bakufu* in 1338. The Muromachi period lasted about 240 years, but its last eighty years or so parallels the Warring States period. For further discussion of the incident at Tōji-in temple, see Walthall, *The Weak Body of a Useless Woman*, pp. 183–202, or her article "Off with their Heads! The Hirata Disciples and the Ashikaga Shoguns," *Monumenta Nipponica* 50.2 (Summer 1995): 137-170.

10. The riverbed of the Kamo River, where the river crosses Sanjō Street in Kyoto. The location became the execution site of criminals in the medieval to early modern periods.

11. The names Kusaka Genzui and Shinagawa Yaichirō are mentioned in the original Japanese text.

12. Another name for the northern part of Honshū. The expression "the thorns and weeds of Michinoku" thus implies the league of domains in the region fighting against the new Imperial government.

13. The number reached approximately two hundred and fifty as of 2010, as mentioned in note 1 of Chapter One.

References

(Cited by Shiba, in this order, for her Japanese original)

Honjō Kumajirō. *Ichijian Kikusha-ni ikō*. Not for sale. 1925.
Yashiro Kumatarō, ed. *Saisho Atsuko toji*. 1926.
Furuya Tomochika, ed. *Joryū bungaku zenshū*. 4 vols. Bungei Shoin, 1919.
Nunomura Yasuhiro. *Meiji ishin to josei*. Ritsumeikan Shppanbu, 1936.
Ichimura Minato. *Matsuo Taseko*. Yamamura Shoin, 1940.
Hara Saihin Sensei Kenshōkai. *Nihon yuiitsu keishū shijin Hara Saihin joshi*. Not for sale. 1958.
Iwai Yoshie. *Tōkaidō gojūsan tsugi*. Chūō Kōron Sha, 1964.
Seikan-in no miya on-nikki. Zoku nihon shiseki kyōkai sōsho. Reprinted. Tokyo Daigaku Shuppankai, 1976.
Imano Nobuo. *Edo no tabi*. Iwanami Shoten, 1986.
Miyazaki Tomihachi, ed. *Aizu Boshin sensō shiryōshū*. Shinjinbutsu Ōraisha, 1991.
Hōjō Hidekazu. *Hyōden Tagami Kikusha-ni*. Private edition, 1992.
Kusudo Yoshiaki. *Ishin no onna*. Mainichi Shimbunsha, 1992.
———. *Zoku ishin no onna*. Mainichi Shimbunsha, 1993.
Bessho Makiko. *"Kotoba" (ekurichūru) o te ni shita shisei no onnatachi*. Orijin Shuppan Center, 1993.
Fukai Jinzō. *Kinsei onnatabi to kaidō kōtsū*. Katsura Shobō, 1995.
Maeda Yoshi. *"Yamanashi Shigako to Haru no michikusa." Fukuoka Jogakuin Tanki Daigaku Kiyō*. No.19. 1983.
———. *"Kutsukake Nakako to Azumaji no nikki." Fukuoka Jogakuin Tanki Daigaku Kiyō*. No.20. 1984.
———. *"Hoashi Misato—sono shōgai to sakuhin—." Fukuoka Jogakuin Tanki Daigaku Kiyō*. No.22. 1985.

————. "*Kinsei kōki no Kita-Chikuzen ni okeru josei no bungei katsudō.*" *Kinsei kenkyū-hen Fukuoka han* 3. *Fukuoka kenshi.* 1988.

Kogure Kiyoko. "*Kinsei ni okeru Josei no sekisho tsūkō ni tsuite.*" In *Ronshū kinsei joseishi.* Yoshikawa Kōbunkan, 1986.

Journal. *Edo-ki onna kō.* 1~ . Katsura Bunko, 1990~

Bibliography

(Cited by the translator)

All Japanese-language texts were published in Tokyo unless otherwise indicated.

Copeland, Rebecca L. *Lost Leaves: Women Writers of Meiji Japan.* Honolulu: University of Hawai'i Press, 2000.

Fister, Patricia. "Female *Bunjin*: The Life of Poet-Painter Ema Saikō." In *Recreating Japanese Women, 1600–1945*, ed. Gail Lee Bernstein. Berkeley: University of California Press, 1991.

Inoue Muneo, and Nakamura Yukihiro, eds. *Fukutake kogo jiten.* Fukutake Shoten, 1988.

Kado Reiko. *Edo joryūbungaku no hakken.* Fujiwara Shoten, 1998.

———, ed. *Ema Saikō shishū "Shōmu ikō."* 2 vols. Kyūko Shoin, 1994.

Kindaichi Haruhiko, and Ikeda Yasaburō, eds. *Gakken kokugo daijiten.* Gakushū Kenkyūsha, 1978.

Koishi Fusako. *Runin Bōtō-ni.* Sakuhinsha, 2008.

Machida Saburō. "*Kamei Nanmei, Shōyō.*" In *Hakatagaku: Hakata chōnin to gakusha no mori*, ed. Asahi Shimbun Fukuoka Honbu. Fukuoka: Ashi Shobō, 1996.

Maeda Yoshi. *Edo jidai joryū bungeishi—tabi nikki hen.* Kasama Shoin, 1998.

———, ed. *Kinsei chihō joryū bungei shūi.* Fukuoka: Tsuru Shobō, 2005.

———, ed. *Kinsei nyonin no tabinikki shū.* Fukuoka: Ashi Shobō, 2001.

Marceau, Lawrence E. *Takebe Ayatari: a Bunjin Bohemian in Early Modern Japan.* Ann Arbor: Center for Japanese Studies, University of Michigan, 2004.

McClain, James L., and Wakita Osamu, eds. *Osaka: The Merchants' Capital of Early Modern Japan.* Ithaca: Cornell University Press, 1999.

Miner, Earl, Hiroko Odagiri, and Robert E. Morrell, eds. *The Princeton Companion to Classical Japanese Literature.* Princeton: Princeton University Press, 1985.

"*Minshū-shi kenkyūkai kaihō*" (Folk History Conference Newsletter), No. 67, May 2009.

Miura Sueo. *Monogatari Akizuki shi.* Akizuki: Akizuki Kyōdokan, 1972.

Morris, Ivan. *The World of the Shining Prince: Court Life in Ancient Japan.* New York: Kodansha International, 1964.

Naramoto Shin'ya, ed. *Nihon no rekishi: Bakumatsu tte nan darō.* PHP, 1990.

Nihon fūzokushi gakkai, ed. *Nihon fūzokushi jiten.* Kōbundō, 1979.

Nomura Shigeo. *Senjimon o yomitoku.* Taishūkan Shoten, 2005.

Robertson, Jennifer. "The Shingaku Woman: Straight from the Heart." In *Recreating Japanese Women, 1600–1945*, ed. Gail Lee Bernstein. Berkeley: University of California Press, 1991.

Sato, Hiroaki. *Breeze through Bamboo: Kanshi of Ema Saikō.* New York: Columbia University Press, 1998.

Shiba Keiko. *Edo-ki no onnatachi ga mita Tōkaidō.* No. 4, *Edo-ki hito bunko.* Katsura Bunko, 2002.

——, ed. *Edo-ki onna kō* 15 vols. Katsura Bunko, 1990–2004.

——, *Kinsei no onna tabinikki jiten.* Tokyōdō Shuppan, 2005.

——, *Kinsei onna tabinikki.* Yoshikawa Kōbunkan, 1997.

——, *Ninomiya Fumi—chichi Sontoku no jigyō ni tsukushita shōgai.* Katsura Bunko, 2001.

——. *"Watashi ni totte no <Edo> no joseishi."* In *Edo no joseishi fōramu*, 1–12. Osaka: Kansai University, 2005.

Shirai Eiji, and Toki Masanori, eds. *Jinja jiten.* 3rd ed. Tōkyōdō Shuppan, 2004.

Shirane, Haruo. *Traces of Dreams: Landscape, Cultural Memory, and the Poetry of Bashō.* Stanford: Stanford University Press, 1998.

Takamure Itsue. *Josei no rekishi.* 4 vols. Kōdansha, 1954–58.

Tanioka Takeo, ed. *Nihon chimei jiten.* 5th ed. Sanseidō, 2007.

Tocco, Martha. "Women's Education in Tokugawa Japan." In *Women and Confucian Cultures in Premodern China, Korea, and Japan.* ed. Dorothy Ko, JaHyun Kim Haboush, and Joan R. Piggott. Berkeley: University of California Press, 2003.

Toyama Susumu, ed. *Bashō bunshū.* No. 17, *Shinchō Nihon koten shūsei.* Shinchōsha, 1978.

Ueda Masaaki, Tsuda Hideo, Nagahara Keiji, Fujii Shōichi, and Fujiwara Akira, eds. *Nihon jinmei jiten.* 5th ed. Sanseidō, 2009.

Vaporis, Constantine Nomikos. *Breaking Barriers: Travel and the State in Early Modern Japan.* Cambridge (Massachusetts): Council on East Asian Studies, Harvard University, 1994.

——. *Tour of Duty: Samurai, Military Service in Edo, and the Culture of Early Modern Japan.* Honolulu: University of Hawai'i Press, 2008.

Walthall, Anne. "The Life Cycle of Farm Women in Tokugawa Japan." In *Recreating Japanese Women, 1600–1945*, ed. Gail Lee Bernstein. Berkeley: University of California Press, 1991.

——. "Off with their Heads! The Hirata Disciples and the Ashikaga Shoguns." *Monumenta Nipponica* 50.2 (Summer 1995): 137–170.

——. *The Weak Body of a Useless Woman: Matsuo Taseko and the Meiji Restoration.* Chicago: The University of Chicago Press, 1998.

Yabuta Yutaka. "Gender and Women's History in the Edo Period." *Rikkyō Institute of Japanese Studies Annual Report* No. 6 (2007): 18–28.

Index